T0268293

101 Things
You Should Know about James Bond
007

101 THINGS
YOU SHOULD KNOW ABOUT

JAMES
BOND

O 7

MICHAEL DÖRFLINGER

SCHIFFER
PUBLISHING

4880 Lower Valley Road · Atglen, PA 19310

Table of Contents

Foreword 7

1 Ian Lancaster Fleming | The Creator of James Bond...................................8
2 Books and Movies | Sometimes There Were Big Differences.......................10
3 Other Bond Authors | Official Imitators on the Market 12
4 The Debut of Ian Fleming's 007 | *Casino Royale*, the First Bond Novel........14
5 Bond's Movie Premiere | *Casino Royale*, the First Bond Movie 16
6 Casino Royale Is Too Much . . . for One James Bond! | The *Casino Royale* Parody 18
7 Lots to Read and Fun at the Movies | The Successful 007 Formula
   Is Easy to Follow 20
8 The Bond of the Twenty-First Century | Daniel Craig as 007.....................22
9 Bond Drives a Ford | A Unique Vehicle for Product Placement 23
10 The Aston Martin DBS | A New Company Car for James Bond 24
11 From Simon Templar to 007 | Roger Moore, the First Englishman to Play Bond..26
12 The Silver Phantom and the Silver Meteor | A Dangerous Train Ride
   with Solitaire 28
13 Telex, Weapon, Timepiece | James Bond and His Watches 30
14 Visiting Drax by Helicopter | Hot Ride with an Erotic Movie Diva..............32
15 The Gondola from Q's Laboratory | Modern Interpretation of a Boat.........33
16 Duel on Sugarloaf Mountain | In This Gondola, 007 Fought for His Life 34
17 Successful Bond Songs | Shirley Bassey Was Entitled to Sing Three Tracks.....36
18 The Two Moonrakers | In the Movie, a Tribute to the Space Shuttle............38
19 Sean Connery | The First "Real" James Bond...40
20 Diamonds Are Forever | Gloriously Politically Incorrect 42
21 Is Killing Really That Much Fun? | The Gay Bad Guys...............................44
22 Movie Bloopers in the Bond Flicks | Detective Work for 007 Fans 46
23 James Bond's Bentley | Ian Fleming's First Choice Was No Mistake 48
24 Q: The Debut of a Legend | Making His First Appearance in
   From Russia with Love...51
25 The Secret Intelligence Service | James Bond Is Working for MI6 52
26 From the Skies with Love | The Helicopters Ridden by 007's Antagonists......54
27 The First EON Movie | James Bond Conquers the Big Screen 56
28 Ian Fleming on the Set | Filming near GoldenEye....................................60
29 Bond the Naval Officer | Diving and Sailing with 007 62
30 The First Bond Car in the Movies | The Sunbeam Alpine Series II...............64

31 Bond's Service Weapon | **The Walther PPK Comes from Germany** 65

32 He Could Be the Best Bond Villain of All | **Gert Fröbe Is Auric Goldfinger**....66

33 Goldfinger's Rolls-Royce | **Even Back Then, This Was a Classic Car** 68

34 Pussy's Flying Circus | **The Bond Girls Phenomenon** 70

35 Falling for James Bond's Charms | **The Ladies Who Get "Turned"** 73

36 The Bond Girl Who Has to Die | In *Goldfinger*, Two Sisters at One Time.....74

37 James Bond and Switzerland | **A Return to His Mother's Homeland** 76

38 The Bond Car Par Excellence | **Thanks to 007, the DB5 Became a Legend**.......78

39 All the Gadgets on the DB5 | **The Secrets of 007's Company Car** 80

40 The Military and 007 | **Military Advisers, the Armed Forces, and Weapons** 84

41 The Flying Bond | **An Early Highlight in *Thunderball*** 86

42 Bond Day and the Headlines | **Media Hype about James Bond, Agent 007** 88

43 The Ravages of Time | **Sean Connery and His Toupee** 90

44 The Spy Who Loved Me | **The Novel Has Nothing to Do with the Movie** 92

45 An Ingenious Sports Car | **Bond's New Car Was Also a Submarine**..............93

46 An Antagonist with a Bite | **One of 007's Best-Known Enemies** 96

47 The Antagonist Is Stronger | **A Common Theme in Bond Movies** 98

48 Lazenby, the Male Model | **From a Beacon of Hope to a Flash in the Pan** 100

49 Winter Sports in the Movies | **James Bond Goes Skiing and Bobsledding**...... 102

50 Blofeld: Bond's Intimate Enemy | **The Man of a Thousand Faces**.............. 104

51 James Bond's Marriages | **The Unforgettable Tracy—
and What of Madeleine?**.. 107

52 James Bond at Work in Japan | **On the Hunt for His Archenemy** 108

53 Bond Raises Toyota to the Peerage | **His Sports Car Was Actually a Yamaha** .. 110

54 Little Nellie Has It Her Way | **Bond Scores Four Aerial Victories in a
Mini Helicopter**.. 112

55 Rumors about Shatterhand | **This Name Comes Up Time and Again** 113

56 Duel of the Players | **Bond on the Hunt for Ian Fleming's Cousin** 114

57 The Weapon of Francisco S. | **Ingenious, Gold, and Temporary**.............. 116

58 Nick Nack | **A Small Enemy Can Also Be Dangerous**............................. 118

59 Cars That Can Even Fly | **Spectacular Vehicle Stunts**............................ 119

60 Where Scaramanga Lived | **They Still Call It James Bond Island Today** 120

61 For Your Eyes Only | **From the Short Story to the Movie**........................ 122

62 Sheena Makes an Appearance | **From 007 to *Miami Vice*?** 123

63 The Real Citroën "Duck" Is Yellow | **. . . and Is Shot Full of Holes** 124

64 A View to a Kill | **This Is Where Opinions Diverge** 126

65 Duran Duran Sings about 007 | **The First Bond Number 1 in the US Charts**. 128

66 Endgame on the Bridge | **The Fight for Life and Death 746 Feet in the Air** ... 129

67 Olga Kurylenko, the Avenging Angel | Daniel Craig Needs a
Quantum of Solace 130

68 Ford Makes a 007 Mobile | Riding Shotgun in the New Ford Ka 132

69 In the Mountains and by the Sea | James Bond Seeks Life 134

70 Mission in Germany | James Bond Visits East and West 136

71 Micro Jet at the Gas Station | The Ultimate Opening-Sequence Gag 138

72 On the Nene Valley Railway | A Little East Germany in Eastern England 140

73 Rumors about the New Bond | From the Shakespearean Stage
to the Wide World 142

74 The Aston Martin V-8 Vantage | Yet Another Carful of Gadgets 144

75 Revenge Instead of a 00 Mission | Probably the Worst Bond Movie Ever 146

76 Pierce Brosnan Takes Over | An Irishman Plays Britain's Top Agent 148

77 Aston Martin vs. Ferrari | An Unequal Duel in *GoldenEye* 150

78 Bungee Jumping Becomes Popular | 007 Jumping a Special Kind of Rope ... 152

79 The High-Tech BMW Brand | In a BMW 750iL, the Driver Never Dies 153

80 Q's BMW—a Self-Driving Car | Remote Control from the Back Seat 154

81 The BMW Z8 | Once Again, the Bavarians Deliver the Company Car 155

82 The Tragic Figure of Elektra King | The Bond Girl as 007's Main Enemy 156

83 A Highland Castle | The Scottish Branch of MI6 158

84 An English Duel | The Aston Martin Vanquish and the Jaguar XKR 160

85 Brosnan's Aston Martin | The Aston Martin V-12 Vanquish 162

86 Jinx | In the Thunderbird 164

87 James Bond, the Patriot | The Union Jack Is Omnipresent 166

88 James Bond's Honda | Through the Bazaar on Two Wheels 167

89 James Bond's Childhood | Born in Wattenscheid 168

90 The Marketing Train Is Rolling | Beating the Drums—Stirred, Not Shaken ... 170

91 Moneypenny in the Field | The Modern Woman Also Goes Galavanting 172

92 The Aston Martin DB10 | Only Ten Were Ever Made and Eight
Were for Shooting the Movie 174

93 Pursuit by Airplane | Sölden's Big Scene in *Spectre* 176

94 And . . . Action! | The 007 Franchise and the Movie Directors 178

95 007 ELEMENTS in Sölden | A Cinematic Installation for Bond 180

96 Commerce and Charity | Bond's Company Car Goes under the Hammer 182

97 The Car for the Fans | The Aston Martin DB9 GT Bond Special Edition 183

98 Bond Cars You Can Play With | Corgi and Lego Accommodate 007 Fans ... 184

99 The James Bond Triumph | The British Motorcycle Manufacturer
Is Part of the Action 186

100 The New Bond Vehicles | The Aston Martin DBS Superleggera and Valhalla 188

101 It All Comes Full Circle | James Bond Is Back in Jamaica 190

Foreword

"I've been expecting you, Mr. Bond!" This is what many fans of the famous secret agent were thinking while they waited for the delayed premiere of the twenty-fifth film in the franchise. But is the greeting using these words actually a quote at all? Was it Blofeld with his white cat in his arms? Or, in fact, Goldfinger or Stromberg? Anyone who watches the movies will listen for them in vain.

There are many myths, facts, and secrets about 007. Clever fans have uncovered so many things that you could write long books about them all. Everyone knows all about Sean Connery, Roger Moore, Daniel Craig, M, Q, and Moneypenny—but who is actually behind the name Ian Fleming? In the first pages of this book you will be able to get to know the creator of the great James Bond. The one hundred chapters that come afterward then follow the chronology of the novels and then of the short stories. Finally, what comes next are chapters on the movies that had no models in Fleming's works, even if they feature motifs that were certainly taken from his works. This opens up new perspectives for watching the movies, which have become far better known around the world than the books are. Because this book was originally published in the secret service of GeraMond Verlag—the Munich publishing house that specializes in technology and traffic and military history—it was my mission to make sure that cars, trains, and airplanes are given plenty of attention. Yet, you don't have to be interested in airplanes and vehicles to come across interesting topics from the world of 007 and his antagonists while reading this paperback book.

Another little note on the design of this title: on the odd-numbered pages, the title of the movie to which the chapter is dedicated is printed next to the page number at the bottom. Each Bond actor is given his own color: Barry Nelson and topics related to the books, Sean Connery, David Niven, George Lazenby, Roger Moore, Timothy Dalton, Pierce Brosnan, and Daniel Craig. There is also color highlighting to make it easy to quickly find the places where the **gadgets** are mentioned.

I hope all Bond fans, old and new, will really enjoy reading this book—and that it helps them pass the time as they wait for new Bond content!

Michael Dörflinger
Augsburg, Germany
Winter 2021

Ian Lancaster Fleming

The Creator of James Bond

On May 28, 1908, joy reigned in the Fleming house in the exclusive London borough of Mayfair: the second of four sons had been born. His parents named him Ian.

The father, Valentine, was Scottish (like James Bond's own father), and the mother, Eve, came from London. Sainte Croix Rose, her French-sounding maiden name, was certainly an inducement for Ian, who later had Bond's mother come from French Switzerland. Valentine, a close friend of Winston Churchill, was a Conservative member of Parliament. He fell in the Battle of the Somme in 1917.

As the son of a prominent family, Ian entered Eton in 1921. Because he wore pomade in his hair and because of his 007-like ways with women, he had to leave school early and was sent to the military academy at Sandhurst. However, he was sent down because he had contracted a venereal disease. If you want to get a look at Ian Fleming, you will find him on page 61.

Years of Education and Agent in the Royal Navy

Following these setbacks, Fleming was educated privately in the town of Kitzbühel, Austria. He lived in the same building where Dexter Smythe—who became the main character of the story "Octopussy"—later lived. A few

There Really Was a James Bond

A secret agent who is publicly known is of no use to his service. So it is not a surprise that the existence of one James Albert Bond was only revealed fifteen years after his death. The diplomat, who was born in Devon, England, in 1928 and died in 2005, is said to have carried out espionage tasks in Warsaw during 1964–65 and was withdrawn from the service after barely one year. Not much more is known about him. Ian Fleming most likely did not know anything about this man, who was twenty years younger than he.

The photograph is from a Polish archive.

Image: Institute of National Remembrance (Instytut Pamieci Narodowej)

semesters of study followed in Geneva and Munich. Because Fleming did not pass the entrance examination for the Foreign Service, he worked as a journalist for Reuters News Agency and *The Times* of London and later as a securities broker.

In May 1939, he was commissioned by the Royal Navy as assistant to the director of Naval Intelligence. Then World War II broke out. Fleming rose to the rank of commander and carried out missions abroad, including in the Soviet Union, the United States, France, and Germany. After the war ended, he worked as head of the foreign news department for a newspaper company for a few years, and it was during this time that he began writing his James Bond novels.

Would you have recognized him? This is what James Bond is supposed to look like. It was Ian Fleming himself who created this drawing.
Image: Collection of Michael Dörflinger

Ian Fleming had seen the world. He had studied in Munich and Geneva, had lived in Kitzbühel, and had traveled throughout Europe. He even traveled around the world for the *Daily Telegraph* newspaper and reported on the most-famous cities in the United States and East Asia. He worked in the Soviet Union as a journalist—and as a spy. He bought himself a house in Jamaica. Along the way, he had collected a large number of maps, brochures, and other materials that he could use for writing his books.

Swimming, Alcohol, Women, and Writing Novels

Ian Fleming had typical "male hobbies" for his era. He smoked and drank a lot, was a hearty eater, and enjoyed diving and fishing—but, most of all, he loved fast cars. Much to his wife's chagrin, he would floor the gas pedal when driving (just recall the drive to the hinterlands of Monaco in *GoldenEye*, starring Pierce Brosnan as Bond). With the fee he earned for the movie rights to *Casino Royale*, he bought a Ford Thunderbird. This model of car appears again and again in the movies.

Secret agents also liked to read his books. The director of the CIA at the time enjoyed leafing through the 007 novels. In fact, he was a good friend of the author.

Ian Fleming died on August 12, 1964, on the twelfth birthday of his son Caspar, who died of an overdose eleven years later. But as the father of 007, Ian Fleming lives on, and his heirs have been extremely successful in safeguarding his legacy.

Books and Movies

Sometimes There Were Big Differences

By 2001, some seventy-five million books by Ian Fleming had been sold worldwide. But it is the iconic movies that have made James Bond truly famous around the globe.

The James Bond movies of the 1960s, produced by EON, were part of a popular genre that allowed you to live the dream of the wide world, at least on the big screen. At the time, many of the world's exotic places were unfamiliar to many people, since long-distance travel was unaffordable for most. So you went to the movies to get a look at Asia, tropical islands, or Monaco.

The classic ingredients—beautiful women, great locations, fast cars, and wild fights—have a greater impact on the big screen than they do on paper. The movies continue to weave the tales of the source material and bring in new elements, such as Q. Often there isn't much left of the plot of Ian Fleming's novel.

The James Bond Books by Ian Fleming

Title	Year of Publication
Casino Royale	1953
Live and Let Die	1954
Moonraker	1955
Diamonds Are Forever	1956
From Russia, with Love	1957
Dr. No	1958
Goldfinger	1959
For Your Eyes Only	1960
Thunderball	1961
The Spy Who Loved Me	1962
On Her Majesty's Secret Service	1963
You Only Live Twice	1964
The Man with the Golden Gun	1965
Octopussy and The Living Daylights	1966

Roger Moore loved long cigars. When he was playing 007, it was necessary to make sure that there were always enough Montecristo No. 2 brand cigars close at hand. It is said that this was even part of his contract agreements.
Image: Allan Warren / CC BY-SA 3.0

Other Bond Authors

Official Imitators on the Market

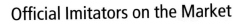

Ian Fleming died very early. He left a fortune, and his heirs sought to make it even larger. The idea of publishing more James Bond books had already came up early on. Geoffrey Jenkins was commissioned to write the first one. He had written a James Bond novel for the Glidrose publishing company in 1966, the plot of which he allegedly had once worked out with Ian Fleming. It is said that he received a fee of £10,000 for consigning this opus to a drawer. Two years later, however, a novel came out after all. Kingsley Amis wrote the book *Colonel Sun* under a pseudonym. In this book, M is kidnapped and Bond sets out to search for him.

A Fictional Biography and a Dictionary

In 1973, John Pearson brought out a biographical novel about James Bond. He provides information about Bond's birthplace and reveals that in the meantime, Bond had married Honeychile Ryder. Eleven years later, Raymond Benson—who later wrote several other fictional works with James Bond as the central character—wrote *The James Bond Bedside Companion*, which is written somewhat in the style of popular research literature. Christopher Wood, who wrote the scripts for *The Spy Who Loved Me* and *Moonraker*, also wrote a novel to accompany both flicks. Raymond Benson did the same thing. In one short story, Benson tells of a son of James Bond, who has the same name. Bond the elder had him with Kissy Suzuki, whom he had married in a mock wedding ceremony in *You Only Live Twice*.

James Bond Authors

Name	Title	Time Frame
Robert Markham (pen name of Kingsley Amis)	*Colonel Sun*	1968
John Pearson	*James Bond : The Authorized Biography of 007*	1973
John Gardner	14 novels, 2 novels based on movies	1981–1996
Raymond Benson	*The James Bond Bedside Companion*, 3 short stories , 6 novels, 3 novels based on movies	1984 1997–2002
Sebastian Faulks	*Devil May Care*	2008
Jeffery Deaver	*Carte Blanche*	2011
William Boyd	*Solo*	2013
Anthony Horowitz	*Trigger Mortis	Forever and a Day*	2015 / 2018
R. D. Mascott (pen name of Arthur Calder-Marshall)	*The Adventures of James Bond Junior: Double-O Three and a Half*	1967
Charlie Higson	Young Bond: 5 novels, 1 short story	2005–09
Kate Westbrook (pen name of Samantha Weinberg)	The Moneypenny Diaries: 3 novels, 2 short stories	2005–08

Jeffery Deaver presents his new Bond novel *Carte Blanche* to Colour Sergeant Andrew Williams of the Royal Marine Commando Force. The lady on the left is Chesca Miles, a model who can also be booked for motorcycle stunts. *Image: Dominic Fraser / Newspress*

The most prolific author in the 007 universe was John Gardner, who authored sixteen novels. The idea to turn M into a woman came to him out of the blue. Gardner was followed by several authors, who created new Bond adventures on behalf of the publisher.

The Moneypenny Diaries and Bond's Youthful Experiences

The first volumes of these two series were published in 2005. Both of them approach the James Bond character from a special perspective. One series was supposed to be written as a trilogy in which Miss Moneypenny's diary entries are collected. She was to report about her private encounters with 007 in these volumes. The other series tells of the adventures of a young James Bond, at school in Eton. Ploys of this kind have had repeated success in other popular franchises, at least since the appearance of *The Adventures of Young Indiana Jones* in the 1990s.

Steve Cole has been continuing the series involving the young Bond since 2015. And then, there are all kinds of nonfiction books about various aspects of the 007 theme. Above all, the Bond cars have proved to be a popular topic. There are even books about his martinis: Would you prefer shaken, not stirred?

The Debut of Ian Fleming's 007

Casino Royale, the First Bond Novel

It was on February 17, 1952, that Ian Fleming struck the first typewriter key for his novel *Casino Royale* at his GoldenEye private villa in Jamaica. He wrote about a secret agent who has a somewhat unusual assignment: he is supposed to ruin an agent from the opposite side when playing cards and, thus, eliminate him. The villain had invested a lot of Russian money in a chain of brothels, but a new law had banned prostitution in France. His ruin is imminent. Bond was ultimately able to defeat him at the casino table.

"He was a secret agent, and still alive thanks to his exact attention to the detail of his profession": Fleming is guided by this maxim. He describes in great detail how Bond brushes his teeth, and what exactly he has for breakfast. Fleming also mentions brand names in order to set the scene realistically. In many ways, you can recognize the model of the hard-boiled crime novels from the United States. Themes emerge from the reservoir of espionage, secret dossiers, intrigues by the Soviets, and lurking antagonists who eavesdrop on the hero or want to eliminate him.

Bond, of course, is a master of all the agent tricks. Fleming's first Bond is a rather brooding type, an antihero of the kind that was especially popular in the novels of the postwar era. 007 likes to demonstrate his good taste when dining and drinking. But when in danger, he is not the shining hero that both Sean Connery or Roger Moore were. He really has to suffer—and survives only by the skin of his teeth after an hour of torture. Hero and villain: these maxims very quickly get mixed up in the novels. In the end, even Bond's beloved Vesper Lynd is a traitor.

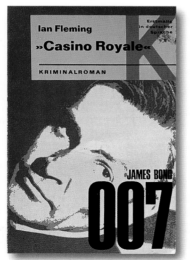

Sean Connery never made a movie based on the novel *Casino Royale*. Nevertheless, you can see him on the cover of this German-language edition. His face is a "draw" for readers because of his successful movies.
Image: Michael Dörflinger

Ian Fleming wrote his first Bond novel in just one month. Many aspects of his own life were incorporated into the plot. *Image: Alan Levine*

Felix Leiter, Bond's Contact Man at the CIA

Felix Leiter, 007's American friend and colleague, has taken part in twelve Bond movies so far and usually has been played by a different actor each time. It wasn't until *Casino Royale* in 2006 that African American actor Jeffrey Wright established himself in the role. Before that, Leiter was white—with one exception: in the unofficial 007 flick *Never Say Never Again*, he was interpreted by an actor of color. Ian Fleming took the name from his American friend Thomas Leiter.

Felix gives Bond the financial support he needs so that he can beat Le Chiffre at the card game. Leiter reappears in the novel *Live and Let Die*, which shows 007 in New York City, where Mr. Big's empire is located. This time, however, Leiter falls into the clutches of the villain Robber, who throws him to the sharks. Leiter is mutilated, but it seems he doesn't taste very good and survives. He also plays an important role in Fleming's last novel, *The Man with the Golden Gun*. He has hired himself out, posing as a hotel clerk at Scaramanga's hotel, and helps Bond take the villain out. In the movies, he repeatedly appears as a rescuer in emergency situations, or he provides Bond with important information and tools. But in *License to Kill*, his luck finally runs out. His wife, whom he has just married, is murdered and now also ends up among the sharks. Bond sets out to avenge this attack. In two of the movies, Leiter is replaced by the CIA man Jack Wade.

Bond's Movie Premiere

Casino Royale, the First Bond Movie

Just a year after the novel was first published, it was also made into a movie—in the United States. That says everything that needs to be said about the terrific success of Ian Fleming's first novel. The black-and-white made-for-television movie *Casino Royale* was produced for the *Climax!* crime series. The producers had turned Bond into a Yank without further ado. CIA man Felix Leiter, in contrast, became an Englishman and was given the first name Clarence. The female part was played by Valerie Mathis, who was a former lover of Jimmy Bond. At first, she was in the camp of the villain Le Chiffre but then changed sides and found her way back to Bond.

The First German-Speaking Bond Villain

The production followed the plot of the novel to the extent that Bond's mission is to beat the criminal Le Chiffre, who wants to make up for his gambling losses, at a card game. Which brings us to the best part of the entire movie: Peter Lorre. The way he plays the disgusting gangster, surrounded by his

Barry Nelson is Jimmy Bond, an American secret agent.
Image: Collection of Michael Dörflinger

henchmen and alternating between being sleazily submissive and mean, displays the talent of this great actor. Lorre had become a star in Germany after his role in *M—eine Stadt sucht den Mörder* (English title: *M*). In Hollywood, he had a hard time at first. This is the tragedy of the exile who had to flee from the Nazis and struggled with the language in a foreign country. It was in such movies as the Mr. Moto series and *Casablanca* that he ultimately also made his breakthrough in the United States. The American James Bond, Barry Nelson, struggles his way through the flick, never exuding any charisma. Linda Christian, who played the female lead, was a former lover of Errol Flynn and was married to Tyrone Power during the filming. Her daughter was Romina Power.

This television movie was a "chamber drama" that wasn't able to enthrall its audience, and the mass-produced piece certainly didn't excite Ian Fleming either. The small-screen movie disappeared for many years and only resurfaced in 1981, when a film historian discovered a copy of the television flick.

The Opening Sequence: Looking Down the Barrel of a Pistol

It is one of the most famous movie title sequences in cinematic history: the barrel of a pistol that is seeking a target. A man walks across the screen from right to left. Before the pistol holder can shoot, his antagonist makes a quick turn and fires from the hip. The barrel falters and blood flows downward. In *Quantum of Solace*, this sequence comes only at the end. It has frequently been copied and used for jokes, such as the one in the image above. This opening sequence was already used in a rudimentary form for the credits in the first Bond movie. There, however, you are looking through the lens of a camera, and instead of the figure of 007, the names of the actors appear. In the first movies, the shooting Bond was played by stuntman Bob Simmons because Sean Connery had not yet signed a contract.
Image: Nico Suykens

Casino Royale Is Too Much . . . for One James Bond!

The *Casino Royale* Parody

During the 1960s, there were lots of jazzy, trendy, and colorful comedies, all of which ended in a wild finale—a crazy race, a huge brawl, or a big foam party. And the brilliant Peter Sellers, who shuffled off this mortal coil far too soon, is always part of the scene. It goes without saying that he could not have been left out of this tribute to Ian Fleming made by famous artists (it was a Famous Artists Production). Sellers plays Evelyn Tremble, a crafty card player who is supposed to steal the money from the villain Le Chiffre, alias Orson Welles, in the Casino Royale. This plot story line is the same as in the novel. Tremble is given a few gadgets by Q—played by Geoffrey Bayldon, who later played the Catweazle—such as his safety vest, so that he can make his appearance in the casino as James Bond. The whole thing develops into a brilliant parody of the scenes between Q and Bond that occur in the official franchise movies.

A Turbulent Comedy

The movie had six directors and the same number of scriptwriters, including Wolf Mankowitz, who had worked on the script for *Dr. No*. John Houston, one of the directors, made his appearance on the screen as M. However, he dies in the beginning of the movie, and Bond drives his mortal remains—a toupee (an allusion to Sean Connery?)—to his widow in Scotland. She is played by Deborah Kerr, who is able to put her Scottish dialect to full use in this role. During his visit to Scotland, agents of SMERSH, the Soviet counterintelligence agency, attack Bond by using remote-controlled snow grouse (ptarmigans).

In a total anachronism, the James Bond played by David Niven has a daughter, whose mother was Mata Hari. The poor daughter was kidnapped from London by using a UFO, with the villain Dr. Noah behind the operation.

The role of Vesper Lynd was taken on by Ursula Andress, the first Bond girl from *Dr. No*. She had almost appeared with David Niven back then, because Ian Fleming had Niven on his radar for the role of James Bond. Niven was one of his favorite actors. Andress had a very special gadget for her weapon: a submachine gun built into a bagpipe. After all, it's often the case that the villains

This image shows a tram, likely in a city in the Netherlands, advertising the "most colorful James Bond movie in the world" on December 19, 1967. Of course, there is a Bond girl to be found here too. *Image: Joost Evers / Anefo*

have better equipment at their disposal than any Q can put together. By the way: At that time, Peter Sellers was married to Britt Ekland. Seven years later, Ekland played the role of Mary Goodnight, who was the one able to destroy the estate of the man with the golden gun.

Le Chiffre was working for SMERSH, the Soviet secret intelligence organization, which had the aim of killing enemy spies. In the movie, the organization's "base camp" is in the casino. As it turns out, the coscreenwriter Woody Allen—who plays the nephew, Jimmy Bond—is the boss. In any case, he has his own totally different, rather personal goals. To achieve them, he developed a virus that makes all women beautiful and makes all the men who are taller than 4 feet, 6 inches die, which will leave him as the tallest man who gets all the girls. This plan doesn't work, of course, and the movie ends in a brawl with an explosion to follow.

Zeitgeist and Pop

This movie is also a treat for movie buffs, because they can look for the whole range of stars playing minor roles or making cameo appearances. These included the British racing idol Stirling Moss—as a chauffeur. At times, the movie makes the impression of being a series of experiments for chaos theory. Many Bond fans don't know what to make of the movie, while others are more enthusiastic.

Lots to Read and Fun at the Movies

The Successful 007 Formula Is Easy to Follow

7

Some 850 million copies—Ian Fleming could only dream of this level of circulation (and the author of this book is doing the same). Jerry Cotton, protagonist of the paperbacks shown above, is the most successful crime fiction character in the German-speaking world. Thousands of copies have been published to date, and more than a hundred authors are writing in the first person under the pseudonym of Jerry Cotton. He's not a secret agent; instead, he's an FBI agent. Yet, his adventures are just as exciting as those of James Bond. The similarity of the names is certainly no coincidence. During the 1960s, a franchise of Jerry Cotton movies was shot in Germany that was based on the James Bond movies. These movies also feature a sizzling musical theme that is always to be heard when the mission leads to success. Jerry always drives a red Jaguar E-Type and has a good friend who energetically helps him in his operations.

Two Jerry Cotton paperbacks from the 1960s. The FBI man struck home with the spirit of the times, and some of his missions were made into movies, which included a lot of references to 007.
Image: Michael Dörflinger

After the First World War, the agent theme was explored over and over again, both in movies and books. The first hero of a "secret agent" book series comes from England, like James Bond. Peter Cheyney wrote the novel *This Man Is Dangerous*, with Lemmy Caution as its main character, in 1936. In 1953, filming started on a French franchise of eight Lemmy Caution movies, with Eddie Constantine in the main role. It boasted all the features familiar to us: a mysterious plot featuring beautiful women, alcohol, cigarettes, and brawls with fierce enemies. Could it be that Ian Fleming also saw these movies? During the Cold War era, secret intelligence service was an omnipresent topic. Time and again, everyone would read about unmasked enemy spies in the newspapers. Since the 1960s, the novels of John le Carré have been keeping readers in suspense with their very realistic descriptions. The author himself had worked for MI6 and was therefore a real "insider." Many of his novels were made into movies, and the first one was a sensation: *The Spy Who Came in from the Cold* with Richard Burton and Oskar Werner.

The cinematic success of James Bond became a popular way to make money, especially when giving the material a mocking, flippant treatment. This began as early as 1964 in the United Kingdom with *Carry On Spying*, part of the famous franchise of *Carry On* movies that ranged over the whole spectrum of movie genres, almost always featuring the same group of actors.

James Bond Plays a Parody of Himself

It wasn't just that entire movies were filmed as secret-agent comedies. Other movies also often included allusions to the Bond movies that everyone would get. Roger Moore even caricatured himself: in the 1981 action comedy *The Cannonball Run*, he plays Seymour Goldfarb Jr., who thinks he's an irresistible womanizer and drives an Aston Martin DB5 equipped with all sorts of gadgets.

In the *Get Smart* television series (1965–70), Maxwell Smart, Agent 86, fights against agents of KAOS. Rowan Atkinson's three *Johnny English* movies skillfully parody the 007 franchise. Neal Purvis and Robert Wade, the scriptwriters for the first installment, are part of the team of writers for the Bond movies. Johnny English is actually a total klutz, but happy coincidences ultimately take him to his goal. He always has an "English girl" by his side and—as if it could be otherwise—drives an Aston Martin. In the tradition of *The Naked Gun: From the Files of Police Squad!* comes the movie *Spy Hard*, featuring *Naked Gun* star Leslie Nielsen. *OSS 117: Cairo, Nest of Spies* (2006), from France and starring the impressive Jean Dujardin, was a successful parody of the Sean Connery movies.

The Bond of the
Twenty-First Century

Daniel Craig as 007

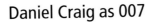

8

The first Bond novel has been filmed three times. The third version was much closer to the original novel, even when the action scenes in particular are unprecedented. *Casino Royale* was the debut of Daniel Craig as Bond, though many would have liked to see him in the role of the Bond villain. He is a brooding Bond, who has a lot to suffer— and thus is much closer to the main character of this Fleming opus, at least. The plot of the movie roughly follows that of the novel. That goes down to the last detail, such as the villain Le Chiffre using a benzedrine inhaler. Right in his very first appearance, Craig's James Bond meets the fate of Felix Lazenby and is unable to prevent the death of his lover, in his case Vesper Lynd. This loss continues to plague him in the next episode, but he is also unsettled because she lied to him and betrayed him. Q and Miss Moneypenny are not on the cast list. Bond has to settle for M, who continues to be played by Judi Dench.

The actor who plays James Bond has become more and more of a brand ambassador. Here, Daniel Craig is posing in a photo call for Range Rover. *Image: Newspress*

James Bond was the first person to drive a 2007 Ford Mondeo. This vehicle, bearing Bahamas license plates from the movie, was a prototype assembled by hand. *Image: Ford/Newspress*

Bond Drives a Ford

A Unique Vehicle for Product Placement

In the Bahamas, 007 drives a rental car that actually wasn't available. The new Ford Mondeo existed only on the drawing board. More than twenty staff workers at the strictly guarded workshops of the Ford Design Center in Cologne, Germany, assembled the car by hand, virtually from scratch, in around two months. It was the prototype of the new model generation, and until then, it had existed only in the minds of the developers. Shrouded in as much secrecy as if it had been transported by the Secret Service, the car finally got to its place of action. This Ford "Bondeo" is painted "tonic blue"—a color with a name that certainly pleased 007, at least. He would likely have preferred some gin to mix with it, more than its automatic transmission. The efforts of the Ford workers paid off. James Bond was able to drive from the airport to his hotel, where he of course arrives unscathed. There are no devious chauffeurs like those in *Dr. No*. Driving a Ford means driving safely—and, no, the author and publisher did not get anything in return for this product placement.

The Aston Martin DBS

A New Company Car for James Bond

A year before the car was launched on the market, 007 was already the owner of an Aston Martin DBS, with a V-12 engine with a displacement of 5.9 liters. Even without such extras as the defibrillator Q provides or the special compartment in the glove box for Bond's Walther P99 on board, a car like this would cost a quarter of a million dollars.

CASINO ROYALE

The Aston Martin DBS

Production period:	2007–2012
Power output:	380 kW
Length:	185.9 inches (4,721 mm)
Height:	50.4 inches (1,280 mm)
Width:	75 inches (1,905 mm)
Top speed:	190 mph (305 km/h)

Image: Newspress

From Simon Templar to 007
Roger Moore, the First Englishman to Play Bond

11

According to the producer Albert Broccoli, they had already had an eye on Roger Moore to become the first EON James Bond, but he was then dismissed because he was considered too young and just a little too handsome. Even in 1969, when Sean Connery no longer wanted to play the role, Moore's name was still on the list. Yet, it took until 1973 for Roger Moore to finally slip into the role of 007, and he immediately emerged on the screen with a bang. In *Live and Let Die*, M and Moneypenny are looking for Bond in his apartment, and they nearly discover the presence of a pretty Italian agent. In his first case, Moore's Bond has a brush with two popular movie themes of his times: the genre of blaxploitation and the fascination with voodoo and zombies. One of the most legendary 007 scenes to this day is the one in which Bond is imprisoned by the villain Tee Hee on an island in a lake full of crocodiles, and he is able to save himself by boldly running right across the backs of the crocodiles to the land. He uses some gadgets, such as a shoe brush that is a radio, a bug detector, and a compressed air cartridge that bursts Dr. Kananga open. His antagonists have much more creative tools at hand: a flute that doubles as a radio, Tee Hee's prosthetic arm, and Dr. Kananga's car that can shoot poisoned arrows.

An Experienced Detective and Gentleman

Roger Moore was practically already "an expert," because just one day before the premiere of *Dr. No*, the first episode of him as *The Saint* was launched on British television. Some 118 episodes of the television series were filmed, up until 1969. In *The Saint*, Roger Moore played the elegant English adventurer Simon Templar, a mixture of master thief, detective, and secret agent. Because Jaguar did not want to make an E-Type available for the series, Simon Templar got a fancy Volvo P1800 with the license plate number ST 1. In between that TV series and James Bond, Moore again enjoyed himself playing a globetrotting millionaire playboy and a kind of detective along with Tony Curtis in the cult TV series *The Persuaders!* In this show, he drives a Bahama-yellow Aston Martin DBS, the same car that George Lazenby drove when he played Bond. This model has nothing to do with the car shown on page 24.

Roger Moore also drove a sports car in *The Saint*. This time it was a P1800, which was manufactured between 1961 and 1972. It was manufactured by Jensen Motors Limited in England until 1963—so Simon Templar was not driving a "foreign car." *Image: Volvo*

Volvo P1800 (Jensen)

Production period:	1961–1963
Power output:	66 kW
Length:	171.3 inches (4,350 mm)
Height:	50.4 inches (1,280 mm)
Width:	66.9 inches (1,700 mm)
Top speed:	106 mph (170 km/h)

The Silver Phantom and the Silver Meteor

A Dangerous Train Ride with Solitaire

Taking the train could be very dangerous in Ian Fleming's books. In his second novel, *Live and Let Die*, James Bond travels from New York City to Florida. The beautiful Solitaire came along with him in his hand luggage—she had managed to escape from the clutches of the villain, Mr. Big. The train stood ready to depart at 10:30 a.m. at platform 14 in Pennsylvania Station. It is the Silver Phantom, hitched to a 4,000 hp streamlined diesel locomotive pulling the classically designed rail coaches of the Seaboard Air Line Railroad. The route of Bond's train reads like a vacation trip: it runs from New York City to St. Petersburg, Florida, via Washington, DC; Jacksonville; and Tampa. The name of the train is actually that of a Rolls-Royce model. This might be due to a lapse of memory by Ian Fleming, because the real Seaboard luxury service to the sunny South ran two trains, one of them the Silver Star. In his book, Fleming correctly names the other luxury train, the Silver Meteor. Bond has booked a luxurious compartment in the name of Mr. and Mrs. Bryce.

Ian Fleming gave his Silver Phantom a slightly different paint design. His diesel locomotive was painted with a purple and gold stripe. *Image: Collection of Michael Dörflinger*

SEABOARD RAILWAY'S SILVER METEOR

The two get off the train before the final destination, knowing that Mr. Big's villains are waiting for them. Bond had sensed the danger correctly, because the criminals stop the Silver Phantom after Jacksonville and—in classic American gangster style—use machine guns and hand grenades to shoot up the compartment where they believe their two targets are still hiding, smashing it to pieces.

In the movie *Live and Let Die*, the train initially has no role to play. Bond and Solitaire, however, aren't able to avoid using public transport entirely, because they capture an old double-decker bus to escape the villains. It is only at the end of the movie that the couple takes the train to Washington. Everything comes down to the final fight with Tee Hee, who appears to be all-powerful with his prosthetic arm. But Bond is able to exactly exploit this supposed strength and cuts the wires for the grip so he can then throw the villain out the window.

Bond travels on the Silver Meteor in the novel *Goldfinger* as well. This time he extorts the tickets from Goldfinger after the latter's attempt to cheat and takes Jill Masterson along. She will be killed during the movie when she is covered entirely with gold paint in the Miami hotel. Now things are heading north, however. In 1953, Fleming traveled this route from New York City to St. Petersburg, Florida, in the company of his wife and could thus describe what he experienced himself.

It was in *From Russia with Love* that the first fight in a train compartment was staged on celluloid for the first time. Bond has to combat the killer Red Grant and has practically already lost the struggle when Q's specially equipped suitcase takes him to victory.

The railroad plays a major role in *Octopussy* because the villains want to use it to smuggle an atomic bomb into West Germany. This time, Bond is fighting not only in the train but also on its roof. Doing things in proper style, he doesn't board the train at the station but jumps up onto it from a car. And who doesn't know the train battles with villains in *GoldenEye* (see page 148) and *Spectre* (see page 98)?

"The train sped on down . . . through the mile upon mile of citrus groves."
Image: Ross Photo Service, New York

Telex, Weapon, Timepiece

James Bond and His Watches

13

In *Live and Let Die*, Bond is issued a Rolex Submariner that Q's department has equipped with a powerful electromagnet. It also features a built-in mini circular saw. Bond uses both tools, enabling him to save his own life. 007 also sports this watch in the *Man with the Golden Gun* yet does not use the gadgets. In the opening sequence of *Live and Let Die*, on the other hand, he wears a Pulsar LED digital watch.

The first chronometer with special functions in the history of the 007 franchise was that possessed by the assassin Red Grant in *From Russia with Love*. It contains a wire cord that he uses to strangle a Bond double. In any case, the villains often have spectacular gadgets. Just like his creator Ian Fleming, in the early Sean Connery movies 007 always wears a Rolex Submariner Reference 6538. But what all can it do? Display the time. In *Thunderball*, he gets to wear a Breitling Navitimer Reference 806 diving watch, which Q has equipped with an integrated Geiger counter. Agent 007 wears a Gruen Precision 510 in *You Only Live Twice* and *Diamonds Are Forever*. In *Never Say Never Again*, Bond's Rolex features a small, integrated high-performance laser. David Niven and George Lazenby follow this tradition and also sport a Rolex.

After the Rolex Era Come Seiko and Omega

The era of Seiko quartz watches begins in *The Spy Who Loved Me*. The Seiko 0674 LC is capable of receiving telex messages from MI6. The Seiko M354 Memory Bank Calendar worn by Bond in *Moonraker* has a function that lets you shoot poison and explosive darts by contracting your muscles. Bond's watch in *For Your Eyes Only* is a Seiko that can receive messages and even be used to make phone calls. That happens at the end, when Prime Minister Thatcher wants to congratulate him. Using his Seiko G757 Sports 100 in *Octopussy*, Bond can locate objects, and he can even watch television on the Seiko TV-Watch DXA001/002.

The era of the Omega Seamaster Professional 300M, which continues to this day, begins with *GoldenEye*. This timepiece is equipped with a laser and a remote bomb control. In *The World Is Not Enough*, the Omega also comes equipped with a mini winch and a flashlight. Daniel Craig is also able to make good use of his Omega watches. In *Skyfall*, he wears an Omega Seamaster Planet Ocean and an Omega Seamaster Aqua Terra.

James Bond watches are always available for purchase. This Omega Seamaster Aqua Terra 150M James Bond Limited Edition was issued in 2015. *Image: Newspress*

Visiting Drax by Helicopter

Hot Ride with an Erotic Movie Diva

14

In the movie *Moonraker*, the leading villain is building space shuttles instead of a nuclear missile. In the movie, the industrialist Sir Hugo Drax not only is up to date in terms of technology but also displays classic taste. So, he had a chateau torn down in France and rebuilt it true to the original in Nevada. 007 is supposed to visit him to find out who might have stolen one of the space shuttles. Bond arrives at Château de Vaux-le-Vicomte with a very special lady pilot: Corinne Cléry, the actress who played Corinne Dufour and became famous for her role in the sadomasochistic flick *The Story of O*. The poor thing is fated to suffer a bitter death, like so many who get involved in brief affairs with James Bond. In the novel, by the way, Hugo Drax is described by Bond as "a sort of Lonsdale figure." By this he meant an English earl who established rules for some sports. But did this name perhaps play a role in the search for the actor who was to play Drax in the movie? His name, in fact, was Michael Lonsdale . . .

James Bond was flown to the Château de Vaux-le-Vicomte in this Bell 206L Long Ranger; the château can be seen in the background. *Image: ManoSolo13241324 / CC BY-SA 4.0*

The Gondola from Q's Laboratory

Modern Interpretation of a Boat

Bond follows the clue discovered at Drax's residence to a glass factory in Venice. While he is riding in a gondola, another gondola approaches. It is carrying a coffin, in an allusion to the movie *Don't Look Now*. The vampire-like figure who emerges from the second gondola is a knife thrower, who kills Bond's gondolier and then throws knives at Bond himself. Agent 007 kills the killer and, threatened by approaching motor boats, transforms his gondola into a speedboat at the push of a button. It finally lands at St. Mark's Square and then sails away in the form of an air cushion vehicle. The idea for such a boat came from Ken Adam and was taken up again in *The World Is Not Enough*. In this movie, Bond sails Q's black speedboat through the streets of London and even through a restaurant. The so-called Bondola was broken up after the filming.

Venice has a role to play once again in *Casino Royale*. This time, Bond is taking things easier on the traffic front. He sent in his resignation notice by email while in a vacation mood on a motorboat.

A highlight of the movie for some; too much of a good thing for others: a replica of Bond's Venetian gondola, which could be transformed into a hovercraft. *Image: Kigsz / CC BY-SA 4.0*

Duel on Sugarloaf Mountain

In This Gondola, 007 Fought for His Life

16

While James Bond doesn't even leave the United Kingdom in the novel version of *Moonraker*, he manages to get around quite a bit more in the movie. In terms of travel technology, the flight in the legendary Concorde to Rio de Janeiro was definitely a highlight. There, 007 follows clues about the activities of his antagonist, Sir Hugo Drax. What does everyone think of when they hear about Rio?

Right: the Copacabana, the Rio Carnival, and Sugarloaf Mountain. And classy, suntanned samba beauties. As luck would have it, Bond is immediately assigned an assistant of this caliber in the form of Manuela. But there is no advantage without some disadvantage: The now-all-too-well-known Jaws (see page 96) is also in the Brazilian metropolis. His attempt to attack Manuela fails, however, because he is pulled along by some celebrating Carnivalists.

Looking through binoculars from Sugarloaf Mountain, it is possible to watch the airport and the activities of the Drax company. Agent 007 is not the only one who is aware of that. Dr. Holly Goodhead, the engineer working for

The new cable car was completed in 1972. It has two gondolas that can each accommodate sixty-five passengers. This is still the one featured in *Moonraker*. Image: Halley Pacheco de Oliveira / CC BY-SA

Sugarloaf Mountain (Pão de Açúca) is one of the landmarks of Rio de Janeiro. It is 1,300 feet (396 meters) high.
Image: Kathrin Natterer

Drax who is actually from the CIA, is also keeping an eye on the traffic. The pleasant encounter she has with James Bond soon turns into a nightmare.

While they are taking the gondola down, Jaws is riding up. They meet in the middle. An accomplice has stopped the cable car. A fierce fight breaks out on the roof of a gondola. The good guys win, and Jaws races with the gondola to the valley

View of the cable car to Sugarloaf Mountain.
Image: Tina Kayser / Pixelio.de

station. But this hellish trip still comes to a happy end for the villain: Jaws meets Dolly, the little blonde with pigtails, and immediately falls in love with her.

The History of the Cable Car

It is popularly christened "O Bondinho" by the Brazilians—but, no, not because of 007! The words simply mean "the cable car." The cable car to Sugarloaf Mountain was opened in 1913. It was replaced in 1972 by today's large gondola lift, and two new gondolas were procured in 2008.

Successful Bond Songs
Shirley Bassey Was Entitled to Sing Three Tracks

With *Moonraker*, Shirley Bassey was able to celebrate winning her triple prize: she was the first and only person to sing the title song for three Bond movies. Before that, she had already recorded the legendary themes for *Goldfinger* and *Diamonds Are Forever*. She is the only one to sing more than one theme song, in any case. Since the movie featuring the legendary Gert Fröbe as Goldfinger, the songs have practically always been set to symbolistic title sequences by Maurice Binder or Daniel Kleinman. The "Goldfinger" track was the first to hit the charts in the United States, reaching no. 8. Paul McCartney and Wings climbed the charts to second place in the United States with "Live and Let Die." Carly Simon achieved the same in 1977.

Dusty Springfield's brilliant song "The Look of Love" is included on the soundtrack of the 1967 version of *Casino Royale* and is heard as an instrumental over and over again. It was nominated for an Oscar but lost to the theme song from *Doctor Doolittle*. The *Casino Royale* theme song was an instrumental by Herb Alpert. The only other time that a Bond movie featured a theme song that didn't have vocals was for *On Her Majesty's Secret Service*. One unusual circumstance is *From Russia with Love*, in which the Bond theme song is heard only during the closing credits. As far as I—and many other 007 fans—am concerned, the best Bond theme song was sung by Scottish singer/songwriter Sheena Easton (see page 123). The *For Your Eyes Only* theme was the first Bond song to top a hit

Who Sang the Bond Title Songs	
Interpreter	**Movie**
Matt Monro	*From Russia with Love*
Shirley Bassey	*Goldfinger*
Tom Jones	*Thunderball*
Nancy Sinatra	*You Only Live Twice*
Herb Alpert & the Tijuana Brass	*Casino Royale (1967)*
Shirley Bassey	*Diamonds Are Forever*
Paul McCartney & Wings	*Live and Let Die*
Lulu	*The Man with the Golden Gun*
Carly Simon	*The Spy Who Loved Me*
Shirley Bassey	*Moonraker*
Sheena Easton	*For Your Eyes Only*
Rita Coolidge	*Octopussy*
Lani Hall	*Never Say Never Again*
Duran Duran	*A View to a Kill*
A-ha	*The Living Daylights*
Gladys Knight	*License to Kill*
Tina Turner	*GoldenEye*
Sheryl Crow	*Tomorrow Never Dies*
Garbage	*The World Is Not Enough*
Madonna	*Die Another Day*
Chris Cornell	*Casino Royale*
Alicia Keys and Jack White	*Quantum of Solace*
Adele	*Skyfall*
Sam Smith	*Spectre*
Billie Eilish	*No Time to Die*

The album including the movie music for *Goldfinger* earned the Gold Record Award. Shirley Bassey's theme song is still considered one of the best Bond songs.
Image: Steven Lek / CC BY-SA.4.0

parade. It reached first place in Switzerland and other countries. The next Bond song, "All Time High," which was sung by Rita Coolidge, who tends to be more in country music territory, was very similar to Sheena Easton's track but not nearly as successful.

Duran Duran managed the feat of playing their way to the top in the United States. In 2012, Adele's "Skyfall" became the first Bond song to win an Oscar. In the British charts, the two most recent songs have taken first place. Due to the coronavirus pandemic, Billie Eilish's "No Time to Die" came out in February 2020—long before the film arrived in the movie theaters.

The Two Moonrakers

In the Movie, a Tribute to the Space Shuttle

18

With the launch of the space shuttle, NASA had broken new ground in space travel. A spacecraft capable of landing by itself, like an airplane, after reentering the Earth's atmosphere was considered a sensation at the time. The special feature of this technology was that the shuttle could be used again. The first shuttle completed its maiden flight on August 12, 1977—exactly thirteen years to the day after Ian Fleming's death. (It is certainly the case that no movie buff needs to be told why the orbiter was named the *Enterprise*.) The launch was made in an unusual way, with a Boeing 747 transporting the shuttle on its roof to the appropriate altitude, and only then was the spacecraft released. A flight like this—with the 747 used as a transport—is shown at the beginning of the Bond movie. This is when gangsters steal the shuttle, named the *Moonraker*. However, the *Enterprise* was not yet capable of making a flight into space. The first model capable of space flight, the *Columbia*, was delivered to NASA in March 1979.

Quick Reaction to an Exciting Theme

For Your Eyes Only was announced as the next Bond flick in the closing credits for *The Spy Who Loved Me*. But with the development of the space shuttles, everyone was talking about space travel again, for the first time following the first moon landing. On top of that, movie fans were in the throes of *Star Wars* fever. Therefore, it made sense to send James Bond into space, too, and to shoot *Moonraker* before the first space flight of a space shuttle, if that could be done!

And, indeed, Drax and Bond beat the real space shuttle to the punch. It took more than a year before things all came together: after several postponed dates, the first reusable spacecraft in the world was launched on April 12, 1981.

The screenwriters certainly had a lot of fun incorporating all sorts of allusions to well-known science fiction movies into *Moonraker*. These included the sound sequence of the code that Bond needs for the door to the secret lab. The five-note sequence (G-A-F-F-C) was lifted from *Close Encounters of the Third Kind*, which came out in 1977.

That movie is famous for its gadgets and all kinds of technical gimmicks. For some fans it was all too much, which is why they rowed things back a bit for the next movie. Holly's gadgets include an appointment planner that shoots

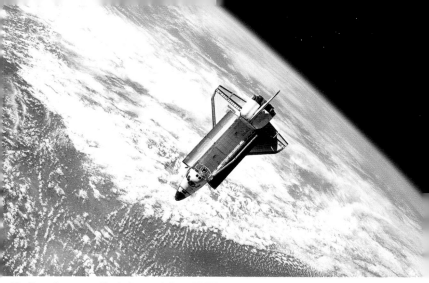

The Moonraker space orbiter looks very similar to NASA's space shuttle, which had not been launched yet at the time the movie was made. *Image: NASA*

poison darts and a handbag that functions as a radio. Besides his watches, Bond can make use of a safe cracker that has an x-ray function. He also has a converted small motorboat made by the Glastron Company, outfitted with water mines, torpedoes, and a kite glider. Along with all this came a ballpoint pen including a lethal injection and a mini camera. Not to be forgotten were the convertible gondola and, finally, the space orbiter taking them to Hugo Drax's space station.

In the Book, It Was a Nuclear Missile

When Ian Fleming was writing in 1955, of course no one was thinking about space travel. In Fleming's novel, Drax donates a nuclear missile to the British, which bears the name Moonraker. Like the industrialist Gustav Graves in the later movie *Die Another Day*, Hugo Drax is very popular among the population and is knighted by the queen, but the man has a dark secret. This hatred-ridden man is planning to use his nuclear missile to destroy London. He and his special space scientists are Nazis from Germany. The finale can be seen on film in *The Spy Who Loved Me*. In that movie, the 007 antagonist Karl Stromberg ties Bond and his girl to the belly of a rocket that is about to launch. As in the book, they are able to break free just in time. In this movie, too, the nuclear missiles are reprogrammed and strike the enemy submarines; in the book, it is that of the fleeing Drax.

Sean Connery

The First "Real" James Bond

19

Most people thought *Diamonds Are Forever* would really be the last movie featuring the popular James Bond actor Sean Connery. But after standing in once again for the disappointing George Lazenby to make *Diamonds Are Forever*, Connery said yes to playing Bond again twelve years later. For many, Sean Connery is considered the James Bond of all Bonds. In fact, he is the type of man Ian Fleming had imagined Bond to be. At the beginning, he might have been a bit wooden at times, but he improved his acting performance enormously. Connery had that certain something that made it believable that he would always end up with the Bond girls. Perhaps no scene better conveys his character than the one during the opening sequence of *Goldfinger* where he comes out of the water wearing a wetsuit, takes it off, and emerges wearing his dinner jacket underneath it—a flower in his buttonhole. Now the mission can begin!

This is the way Sean Connery became famous as James Bond: casual, with a somewhat animalistic effect; a sporty bon vivant propping himself up on his Aston Martin DB5. *Image: Aston Martin*

Sean Connery during his *Goldfinger* times. *Image: ETH University Library Zurich, Picture Archive / Comet Photo AG / CC BY-SA 4.0*

Diamonds Are Forever

Gloriously Politically Incorrect

20

This movie is by no means one of the best movies Connery made in the James Bond franchise, but it includes all sorts of ingredients that make it worth watching today. In many scenes, *Diamonds Are Forever* adheres very closely to the original novel. Thus, it is about diamond smuggling, with James Bond bringing the gems to America while disguised as one Peter Franks. Here he meets Tiffany Case, and then there are the two murderers whom he is able to kill at the end, while sailing on an ocean liner. These two are, by the way, named Winter and Kitteridge. In the movie, some character names are abbreviated (see page 44).

Penny was called Plenty O'Toole in the original—which is as raunchy a pun (lots of tools, meaning breasts) as some of 007's other remarks to and about women. In the novel *Casino Royale*, Bond made it very clear just what view he has of women: "Women were for recreation. On a job, they always got in the way and fogged things up with sex and hurt feelings and all the emotional

It looks a bit rickety, but James Bond turned this moon vehicle into an effective getaway vehicle from Willard Whyte's factory. *Image: Lennart Guldbrandsson*

Filming on the Reguliersgracht canal in Amsterdam. The public eagerly followed Bond's arrival in front of Tiffany Case's residence driving a Triumph Stag. *Image: Rob Mieremet / Anefo*

baggage they carried around. One had to look out for them and take care of them." Bond has no problem striking women or even killing them for the sake of the mission, or if the lady were a traitor. In *Diamonds Are Forever*, he has to combat Bambi and Thumper, two athletic women who know a lot about martial arts techniques. The names of these two poolside bathing beauties come from the Disney movie *Bambi*. They may appear to be lascivious but are in fact brutal. These three will certainly not resolve any gender issues.

Even **Gadgets** Were Misused

Q uses his invention to take out the one-armed bandits in Las Vegas. However, he is not interested in the coins he has won. Bond uses a climbing rope he has shot out of a pistol to break into a villa. Agent 007 is able to deceive Tiffany Case by using a fake fingerprint. And then there is Q's voice modulator, which you can use to modify voices in such a way that you sound like another person. Whatever: Ernst Stavro Blofeld, Bond's antagonist, already had such a device long before.

Is Killing Really That Much Fun?

The Gay Bad Guys

21

Apparently, the killer duo Mr. Wint and Mr. Kidd are actually an item in their private life. At one point, Bond makes a direct reference to this situation by saying that Wint's aftershave is "too sweet and too gay." The viewer already had gotten a sense of who the two of them are right at the beginning, when they use a poisonous scorpion to kill a dentist. This pair of villains is just one big cliché, something that made many movie buffs laugh. The contrast to their ice-cold murderous souls makes the two figures extremely fascinating. By the way, the killer executing the murder is always Mr. Wint. Just what does that mean?

Anyone Who Can't Whistle

In his views on homosexuality, Bond, like his creator Ian Fleming, is definitely old school. A passage in *The Man with the Golden Gun* reads quite facetiously, as you can see for yourself. M is studying a psychologist's written memo on the killer Scaramanga, who is assessed, among other things, to likely be a homosexual. One indication, the psychologist writes, is that Scaramanga allegedly cannot whistle, which is considered evidence

The teacher Mrs. Whistler met her undoing because she had smuggled diamonds from South Africa to Holland. Wint and Kidd have prepared a damp grave for her. *Image: Rob Mieremet / Anefo*

The killer pair, Mr. Wint and Mr. Kidd, after their work is done. The man on the right is Putter Smith, a jazz musician. Producer Harry Saltzman had discovered him when he was performing with Thelonious Monk. *Image: Rob Mieremet / Anefo*

of homosexual tendencies. M unconsciously immediately purses his lips to make a test . . . a tone emerges.

A Few Nonchalant Quips at the Right Time

Now we come to an important motif in all the James Bond movies: cracking a corny joke after one of his enemies dies. After the deaths of the two killers at the end of the movie, Bond merely comments coolly, "He certainly left with his tails between his legs." In the opening credits, he sends a message, "Welcome to hell, Blofeld!," after the man he has just killed. Such quips can be found especially in the Sean Connery and Roger Moore movies. For example, when Hugo Drax meets his end, as he is being sent into space, Dr. Holly Goodhead asks, "Where's Drax?" 007 responds, "Oh, he just took a giant step for mankind." Not only are these quips meant to be funny; they are also meant to ensure that Bond does not get the image of an ice-cold killer. In the later flicks, this was no longer considered necessary, which is why Daniel Craig practically never makes any accompanying quips.

Movie Bloopers in the Bond Flicks

Detective Work for 007 Fans

22

One of the highlights of *Diamonds Are Forever* is the car chase through Las Vegas. Bond is at the wheel of a bright-red Ford Mustang Mach 1 and is being chased through the gambling town at night by no fewer than fifty-three police cars. When it appears that he has reached a dead end, he manages to drive his car along a ramp, balancing it on two wheels, and then to drive it at an angle through a narrow pedestrian passage. The only thing that looks odd is that when he drives out the other side, the car is no longer riding on the right wheels, but on the left ones. This was because some of the scenes were shot in America, but a reshoot was done in the United Kingdom. The British actors, who of course drive on the left side of the road, were able to perform this stunt only the wrong way around. No matter—this number sparked a lot of enthusiasm and has found a lot of imitators in movie history.In *Dr. No*, there is a brawl with the traitorous chauffeur in Jamaica. Bond strikes out using his right hand but then is shown hitting the chauffeur with his left. Additionally, at times it appears that the actors have exchanged their cars, because the cars suddenly look different. This is the case with the car of the three blind men in *Dr. No* and with Bond's Aston Martin in *The Living Daylights*, which is still a convertible in Bratislava but then becomes a coupe in the chase scenes on the lake.

Dr. No shows how strong he is by using his metallic hands to crush a statue. It seems that the statue is one of a collection because later another one like it will appear in its place. In *From Russia with Love*, Rosa Klebb keeps changing her hair color like a chameleon, and the same thing happens with such things as flowers, diving goggles, and oxygen cylinders. In *GoldenEye*, the color of the parachutes changes. In *From Russia with Love*, Bond sometimes has a scar and sometimes does not. In *Diamonds Are Forever*, he climbs out of a swimming pool and immediately afterward is seen with his hair dry and combed. He also has the ability, as in *You Only Live Twice*, to first get into a car on the left side and then climb out again on the right later on. In two consecutive scenes, Corinne Dufour is wearing shoes and then boots—and in *Never Say Never Again*, Fatima Blush does it the other way around. She is doing her work wearing boots, but after Bond kills her, there are high heels left lying around. In *In a View to a Kill*, Stacey Sutton also swaps her shoes in San Francisco, and she wears a dress that seems to repair itself.

Bond drives his Ford Mustang into a narrow pedestrian passage balanced on the right wheels—and comes out on the other side, driving on the left wheels. *Image: Newspress*

In *Goldfinger*, the gold-covered Jill Masterson is seen lying in a slightly different position, depending on the setting. What was much more noticeable in this movie, however, was the mistake about Oddjob's bowler hat. When he throws it to decapitate the statue, it flies out of the picture to the right. But the scoundrel picks it up from right next to the disfigured stone lady. One mistake that still always strikes people as funny is the one involving the suddenly missing bullet holes in Bond's Citroën 2CV in *For Your Eyes Only*.

Such movie bloopers are by no means rarities—even in the multimillion-dollar productions made in later years. One classic can be seen in *Casino Royale*, when Daniel Craig enters a password that is different from the one he gave Vesper Lynd. But the wrong password also works. In *Spectre*, the criminals drive into the Rosi Mittermaier Tunnel in Austria, taking the kidnapped Madeleine with them, and then come out of the same side of the tunnel.

Or have you found a spelling mistake somewhere? Bondisti from all over the world keep on uncovering all these mistakes and really have a good time doing it. The moviemakers have now acquired a taste for the bloopers and sometimes hide "smilies"—joking references to earlier versions—in the movie or make cameo appearances as actors in the movie themselves. In *Spectre*, the sign on the safe house reads "Hildebrand Prints & Rarities"—an allusion to Ian Fleming's short story "The Hildebrand Rarity." There's a lot to discover. And that makes it fun to watch the movies more than once.

A Bentley R-Type Continental Drophead Coupe from the novel *Thunderball*. *Image: Newspress*

James Bond's Bentley

Ian Fleming's First Choice Was No Mistake

23

In the initial Fleming novels, James Bond always owned a Bentley. The Bentley 4.5-liter with an Amherst Villiers supercharger, which was purchased in almost new condition in 1933, was a navy-and-gray convertible with a coupe top. It was destroyed in the very first novel, *Casino Royale*, when Le Chiffre's henchmen scattered steel nails on the road and made the Bentley flip over. Its successor, from production year 1933, suffers the same fate in *Moonraker*, because villain Willy Krebs lets loose huge rolls of newsprint onto the Bentley from a truck. M presents Bond with a Bentley Mark VI. Finally, he is the possessor of a Bentley R-Type in *Thunderball*.

This tradition does not continue on film. In *From Russia with Love*, James Bond has only a brief opportunity to use his Bentley. While on a picnic with his lady friend Sylvia Trench, he is contacted via a pager and requested to call MI6; he does this on a car phone. This car is a 1935 Bentley 3.5-liter Drophead Coupe

with a car body made by the Park Ward company. Back then, many makes of automobile delivered only the chassis, and the body was built onto it in your own workshop. Since 1939, Park Ward had been fully owned by Rolls-Royce, which had taken over Bentley in 1931. This is how this cooperation was created.

In the novel *Goldfinger*, Bond got an Aston Martin DB Mark III as his company car. The model used in the movie of the same name was of course the latest, the DB5. That was the end of the Bond Bentleys. Or perhaps not? No, because David Niven also drove a Bentley in his role as Sir James Bond in the earlier version of *Casino Royale*. In *Never Say Never Again*, the filmmakers also reverted to the Bentley. Bond drove a 1937 Bentley 4,5-liter Gurney Nutting to the Shrublands health club; on the road, he gets involved in a race and car chase with the villain Count Lippe. The latter is then liquidated by an associate from his own organization and is thus no longer able to pose a serious danger to 007.

Bentley R-Type Continental	
Production period:	1951–1955
Power output:	110 kW
Length:	200 inches (5,080 mm)
Height:	about 59 inches (1,500 mm)
Width:	69 inches (1,753 mm)
Top speed:	118 mph (190 km/h)

The dialogues between Q and 007 are legendary. Here Q is talking to the British secret agent, portrayed by Roger Moore. For his mission against Hugo Drax in *Moonraker*, Q provides 007 with a device for opening a safe, hidden in a cigarette case. *Image: Picture Alliance*

Q: The Debut of a Legend

Making His First Appearance in *From Russia with Love*

One of the most important innovations made by the Bond movie scriptwriters was to introduce Q, the head of a division dedicated to developing secret weapons, special vehicles, and all kinds of tools for secret agents. Desmond Llewelyn made this role iconic. Fleming already has a Q in *Casino Royale* who is responsible for hotel bookings and train timetables, a genuine quartermaster. His predecessor appeared very briefly in *Dr. No*: Major Boothroyd, a pale figure who appears only briefly and hands 007 a new pistol. It is only with Desmond Llewelyn that Q becomes a character who gains a bigger profile and screen presence as the Bond franchise progresses. In *From Russia with Love*, Bond gets his first **gadget**, a technical gimmick that will save his life when he uses it. It is a briefcase containing a precision rifle he can take apart and a night vision device. It also contains ammunition, a number of gold coins, and a knife. The lock is secured in such a way that a stranger inevitably gets dosed with tear gas.

24

Bond is always poking fun at Q, such as in *Octopussy* when 007 thoroughly enjoys using one of Q's cameras to make a female employee's cleavage appear on the screen. Pierce Brosnan does something similar: he uses the x-ray glasses designed to detect weapons under clothing to examine the lingerie of the women in the room. Bond and Q share a kind of love-hate relationship, and their dialogues are a highlight of any Bond movie. Of course, 007 is always able to immediately make proper use of the devices and cars provided by Q. Pierce Brosnan even shreds the Aston Martin Vanquish user manual to pieces by using it to set off the machine pistols mounted on the car.

With Ben Whishaw playing the modern Q, a bespectacled computer geek, the era of gadgets has unfortunately come to an end: there just aren't any more exploding pens. There is only one pistol that is coded in such a way that only Bond himself can fire it. Full digitization has finally come to MI6; Q lets 007 know that he would be able to do more damage with his laptop.

The Actors Who Played Q	
Desmond Llewelyn	1963–1999
Alec McCowen	1983
John Cleese	1999–2002
Ben Whishaw	since 2012

The Secret Intelligence Service

James Bond Is Working for MI6

25

From Russia with Love is one of the relatively few real secret-agent movies featuring James Bond that takes place during the Cold War. Yet, here too it becomes clear that the main villains are not working for the Warsaw Pact, but on their own account. In some of the Bond adventures, it is the fictional organization of Ernst Stavro Blofeld, Spectre (Special Executive for Counterintelligence, Terrorism, Revenge, Extortion), playing the role of the antagonists. The aim of the mission is to get hold of the Spektor cipher machine (which is called the Lektor machine in the movie) in good old-fashioned secret-agent style. Bond is working for MI6, which has offices in a building on Regent's Park, London, in the novel.

A Symbol of the Old Imperial Era

MI6 has been housed in an imposing building on the Thames since 1995. The building plays an important role in several movies, and, in

Military Intelligence, Section 6, has been at home in this impressive structure on Vauxhall Cross, right on the Thames, since 1995. *Image: Garry Knight / Flickr*

In *Skyfall*, the MI6 building is badly damaged during an attack. Two of Bond's beloved Aston Martins can be seen in the foreground on Vauxhall Bridge. *Image: Aston Martin*

fact, it is even destroyed by an attack. MI6 (Military Intelligence, Section 6) is the British foreign intelligence service, formally the Secret Intelligence Service. It developed out of the Naval Intelligence Division. No wonder, then, that Bond served in the Royal Navy and that M has the rank of admiral. The director of MI6 is actually called "C." It is only in Fleming's works that the front organization of the Secret Service abroad is called the "Universal Exports" company. MI5 is the domestic counterpart of MI6.

The Branches of the Secret Service

Especially in the Roger Moore movies, the screenwriters loved to introduce a branch of MI6 in one of the more exotic locations visited in the plot.

So, MI6 agents could be stationed in an ancient Egyptian temple complex in Abu Simbel, have set up home in the wreck of HMS *Elizabeth* off Hong Kong, or be squatting in a Latin American monastery. Q's department has always come along also, which actually doesn't make sense but makes it possible to stage the wonderful dialogues between 007 and Q.

Finally, another piece of information at which someone or other will smile: since autumn 2020, the head of MI6 has been one Richard Moore . . .

From the Skies with Love

The Helicopters Ridden by 007's Antagonists

26

A helicopter makes its first Bond movie appearance in *From Russia with Love*. Rosa Klebb, alias Lotte Lenya, lands a Hiller UH-12 in a park to check on the killer Red Grant. Lenya plays the Soviet villain brilliantly, and many fans will remember her attack on Bond by using the poisonous barb in her shoe tips. Her helicopter crew, obviously the same people, reappear in this machine later in the movie. This time, the two villains are pursuing the fleeing Bond, who jumps out of his vehicle behind a rock and is ultimately able to use the sniper's rifle from his gadget briefcase to shoot down the helicopter.

A Dangerous Weapon, but No Match for Bond

Helicopter chases subsequently became a popular theme in the movies. In *You Only Live Twice*, the Japanese secret service owns a large Kawasaki Vertol KV107, which carries out a spectacular action. Using his gadget, a

The AS355 Ecureuil 2 is made by Airbus. Elektra King owned two models of this type, one with the registration G-BPPJ. *Image: Jonathan Payne / CC BY-SA 2.0*

powerful magnet, the helicopter pilot picks up Bond's pursuers in their black Toyota Crown, lifts the car into the air, and drops it into the water. The Japanese secret service also has an Aerospatiale Alouette 316B, in which Tiger Tanaka, head of the secret service, and 007 fly to the Ninja school. In the same movie, four Bell 47 G-3s attack James Bond in his small helicopter "Little Nellie" (see page 112). Thanks to his special weapon from Q, he is able to deal with all four without any major problems.

The Hiller UH-12E4. In *From Russia with Love*, Bond is attacked by a machine of this type. *Image: Newspress*

In *The Spy Who Loved Me*, Bond and his Soviet colleague, riding in a Lotus Esprit S1 sports car, are chased by a Bell 206 Jet Ranger helicopter, in which Bond girl Naomi is sitting. Agent 007 drives the car into the water, turns it into a submarine at the push of a button, and doesn't hesitate to shoot Naomi, who is lurking just above the surface of the water.

The Eurocopter Is (Almost) Enough

At the beginning of Pierce Brosnan's debut movie, *GoldenEye*, Bond is unable to prevent the theft of the new Eurocopter Tiger military helicopter—which can withstand the strongest electromagnetic radiation— when it is presented in Monaco. Antagonist Alec Trevelyan later escapes from the train by helicopter with Xenia Onatopp. In this escape, the roof of the rail carriage opens up, and the helicopter emerges. Later, in *The World Is Not Enough*, Elektra King is also in possession of a Eurocopter (known today as an Airbus). She also uses this whirlybird to set her down on skis in the high mountains, to check the pipeline. Bond accompanies her and saves her from members of the Russian nuclear energy antiterrorist unit, who attack in snowmobiles with parachutes. In addition to her two Ecureuil 2s, which you're certain to remember because of the way they saw things up with their circular saws, Elektra also owns a Eurocopter AS-365N Dauphin.

In *Spectre*, Blofeld flees in a Eurocopter AS-365N2 Dauphin 2 but is shot down by 007 firing a pistol. Gustav Graves owns a Notar MD-600N in *Die Another Day*. Jinx and 007 are able to use it to escape from the Antonow An-124, one of the largest transport planes in the world.

The First EON Movie

James Bond Conquers the Big Screen

27

For Ian Fleming, it must have been like getting a Christmas present. His novels were to be made into a movie, and the filming would take place near his estate in Jamaica. They had chosen the adventure featuring the villain Dr. No, although it was actually the sixth volume in the novel series. The action takes place in Jamaica,

where Dr. No has built a high-tech hideout on an offshore island. Given the huge circulation of Ian Fleming's books—thirty million copies had been sold by the time of his death—one could assume that there would be a very good box office response to a movie for the theaters.

The Actors Who Played M	
Bernard Lee	1962–1979
Edward Fox	1983
Robert Brown	1983–1989
Judi Dench	1995–2012
Ralph Fiennes	since 2012

Moneypenny, M, and James Bond. Since *Dr. No*, this trio has almost always been part of the action. Lois Maxwell and Bernard Lee made their mark on these roles. *Image: Picture Alliance*

In fact, this is what happened. The *Dr. No* movie made a profit of nearly $60 million. It premiered on October 5, 1962, and after that, the world of cinema has never been the same. The same was true for Sean Connery and Ursula Andress, who rose to the ranks of world stars. In fact, much of what began with this film still feels up to date sixty years later. It starts with the James Bond theme. This music served as the title song for this movie and would go on to be used over and over again later on. The guitar riff alone gives Bond fans goose bumps. This theme is used again and again by the movie composers when the screen is showing a typical 007 mission. Typical Bond? The piece by Monty Norman actually comes from a musical that the composer had written a few months earlier. Norman is said to have earned just £200 for the piece. The royalties have earned him a lot more.

James Bond displays some agent tricks in *Dr. No*, such as sticking a hair across a closet door so he can see later if someone has searched the room. For the first time he is also armed with a **gadget**: a Geiger counter that he brought along from London. A colleague from the CIA also appears for the first time: Felix Leiter. Bond's superior M and his secretary, Miss Moneypenny, make their debut in *Dr. No*. M, a pipe-smoking admiral, is the director of MI6. Sometimes he makes a big show of being in charge, which subsides somewhat over the course of the franchise. Bernard Lee left a lasting mark on the role. The makers of the franchise took a completely different direction when the former M was given a successor, played by Judi Dench, in *GoldenEye*. The relationship between Dench's M and Bond was mostly one of distrust and mutual dislike, yet there is something unspoken hovering between the two. With Daniel Craig as Bond, this relationship is explored more deeply. Judi Dench said goodbye to her role in *Skyfall*; she is murdered by the villain Raoul Silva before Bond can eliminate him. Silva calls her "Mama." That's weird, because Ian Fleming is said to have called his mother simply "M."

The M in the books is something of a fatherly friend. He and Bond even go to their club together every now and then and play cards. When M sends 007 on a suicide mission, Fleming describes his state of mind. He then drinks a whole bottle of Algerian wine—instead of half a bottle—at lunch in his local pub, appearing irritable and absent-minded. The scriptwriters had come up with something very special for M's secretary, Miss Moneypenny. She is not to be found in the novels, or perhaps only in a rudimentary way in Bond's secretary, Mary Goodnight. Moneypenny adores James Bond. The brief, slightly erotic verbal exchanges between the two are among the highlights of every Bond movie. For many years, Lois Maxwell embodied the lady in M's outer office, who always

Eve Moneypenny has been working for MI6 since *Skyfall*. Her role is a mixture of that of the former secretary of M and Bond's assistant Mary Goodnight, taken from the novels. In *The Man with the Golden Gun*, she puts 007 in danger by making mistakes. *Image: Francois Duhamel / Newspress*

knew how to resolve the differences between the two alpha pack leaders. For example, in *On Her Majesty's Secret Service* she converts Bond's hasty resignation into a vacation. Reportedly, Lois Maxwell might also have played the role of the erotic Sylvia in the casino, but she didn't have an appropriate evening dress. What bad luck! The relationship between the two characters barely changed until a new constellation emerged in *Skyfall*. Played by the young, attractive Naomie Harris, Moneypenny is now also doing fieldwork.

The Moneypennys	
Lois Maxwell	1962–1985
Pamela Salem	1983
Caroline Bliss	1987–1989
Samantha Bond	1995–2002
Naomie Harris	since 2012

It was in *Dr. No* that we would hear for the first time "My name is Bond, James Bond," spoken at the gaming table. In the books, this statement, which has become an iconic catchphrase, is already to be found in *Casino Royale*. The first of many accidents on set also occurred when making *Dr. No*: director Terence Young, a paratrooper himself during World War II, was involved in a helicopter crash but was able to save himself.

Ian Fleming on the Set

Filming near GoldenEye

28

In the second Bond novel, *Live and Let Die*, Jamaica becomes a central movie location. In the book, Fleming described many places in his everyday surroundings.

The sixth in the series, *Dr. No*, in some ways is a continuation of this title. Strangways, Bond's contact person, is murdered, and the trail leads to the infernal Dr. No, whom Bond will take down in the course of the novel. This continuation was made into the first of the 007 movies. The producers worked closely along with Fleming. Some of the filming was done in the immediate vicinity of GoldenEye, Fleming's villa in Jamaica where he wrote his novels. No wonder the writer was keen to follow what was going on right in front of his door. The actress who played Honey Rider certainly made an impression on this aging ladies' man. There are some photos showing him in intense dialogue with the beautiful blond actress. When making *Live and Let Die*, some of the scenes were even shot at GoldenEye. By that time, however, the author was no longer among the living.

Ian Fleming also appeared on location in 1963 during the filming of *From Russia with Love*. This time, he had made a special trip to Istanbul, which he had already visited once before in 1954. There, he meticulously researched the locations for his novel and also got to know the man who would be the role model for his character of Darko Kerim Bey.

If you want to read more about how Fleming lived his life in Jamaica, you should read the book *Octopussy*. The protagonist, Dexter Smythe, is in fact leading a contemplative life on the Caribbean island, which in many details corresponds to Fleming's lifestyle. His boat was named the *Octopussy*.

Ian Fleming in earnest conversation with the first Bond girl, Ursula Andress. Like James Bond's mother, she is Swiss. Would Fleming have liked to slip into the role played by Sean Connery? He even gives her a cameo role in *On Her Majesty's Secret Service*: "And that beautiful girl with the long fair hair at the big table, that is Ursula Andress, the movie star. What a wonderful tan she has!" *Image: Picture Alliance / Capital Pictures | CAP/RFS*

Ian Fleming and His GoldenEye

After World War II, Ian Fleming was able to carry out his plan to build a house on the beach in Jamaica. He spent three months there every year, and starting in 1952 he wrote his James Bond books there. He invited Errol Flynn, Truman Capote, and Princess Margaret to be his guests at the villa. Jamaica was a popular destination for wealthy English people on vacation or for those looking for a place to retire. In 1976, reggae star Bob Marley bought the property. Just one year later, Chris Blackwell, whose mother had once sold the land, acquired it. Blackwell, the founder of Island Records, also welcomed many guests there. Sting was among those who whiled some time away in GoldenEye, and he wrote the famous song "Every Breath You Take" for the Police at Ian Fleming's desk. Today, the villa, together with several outbuildings, is a hotel, and anyone who has enough money can book a room. The best way to get there is to fly by private jet to Ian Fleming International Airport, and from there it is ten minutes by car to GoldenEye.

Bond the Naval Officer

Diving and Sailing with 007

29

In many of the movies, James Bond pursues a villain in a speedboat or is himself hunted by one. That trope started in the first movie, *Dr. No*. Author Ian Fleming was an avid diver, swimmer, and sailor himself, so it's no surprise that we keep getting spoiled time and again by being able to see these exciting scenes on and in the water.

Thunderball is definitely a maritime movie, featuring underwater gliders; the villain Emilio Largo's fast yacht, the *Disco Volante*, which has an enormous top speed of 50 knots; and a battle between opposing divers. Roger Moore, playing James Bond in *For Your Eyes Only*, has to make an involuntary long dive. The plot was based on scenes from the novel *Live and Let Die*. This movie includes a scene in which he and Melina Havelock have to dive together, sharing just one oxygen cylinder and taking turns using the mouthpiece. The villains therefore think they both had drowned.

And there is something else, of course, to also think about: diving and beach scenes always promise the sight of suntanned women wearing skimpy bikinis, another common Bond movie trope.

Underwater scenes and motorboat chases are part of the repertoire of many Bond movies. The characters also do a lot of diving in the novels. *Image: Picture Alliance / dpa | Bert Reisfield*

The First Bond Car in the Movies

The Sunbeam Alpine Series II

30

In Jamaica, James Bond drives a blue Sunbeam Alpine Series II. He is pursued by a black hearse and manages to drive his convertible under a building crane. The pursuers, however, go plunging down the slope and die. "I think they were on their way to a funeral," he tells a road worker in the first of Bond's many flippant remarks when an antagonist dies.

The Sunbeam was rented from one Jennifer Jackson, who lived on Lady Musgrave Road, for £10 a day. Almost twenty thousand of these handsome roadster cars were manufactured between 1960 and 1963. The Sunbeam company of Wolverhampton, in the United Kingdom's Midlands, continued to make cars until 1976.

Sunbeam Alpine II	
Production period	1960–1963
Power output	60 kW
Length:	155 inches (3,937 mm)
Height:	51 inches (1,295 mm)
Width:	61 inches (1,549 mm)
Top speed:	101 mph (163 km/h)

The car that 007 rented was a little lighter in color than this one. Bond delivered in his first car chase in this model. *Image: Newspress / Veloce Publishing*

Ian Fleming chose the Walther PPK to be Bond's service pistol only after a tip-off from a knowledgeable reader. His would have been black, however.
Image: Collection of Michael Dörflinger

Bond's Service Weapon

The Walther PPK Comes from Germany

The literary James Bond was equipped with a Beretta 25-caliber by his creator. In a letter addressed to Fleming by a reader, one Major Boothroyd, the latter criticized this small-caliber weapon, which he dubbed a ladies' pistol, and recommended a Walther PPK. For the on-screen James Bond, this matter had already been taken care of in *Dr. No*, since the quartermaster, Boothroyd, handed him a Walther in M's office. The abbreviation PKK indicates the main use for this weapon: Polizeipistole Kriminal, which translates as "criminal investigation police pistol." Bond remains true to the brand. In *Skyfall*, he is issued a Walther PPK/S, which, thanks to new technology, only he can fire off. The Walther company was founded in 1886 in the eastern German town of Zella-Mehlis. The first Walther PPK was manufactured in 1931. It developed into an international bestseller, especially among police forces and for anyone who wanted to carry a concealed weapon. After World War II, the company started production again in Ulm in southwestern Germany. This is also the place where Bond's service weapon was made.

31

He Could Be the Best Bond Villain of All

Gert Fröbe Is Auric Goldfinger

Compared to other movies, *Goldfinger* sticks very closely to the novel. It starts with a card game in Miami and ends in a finale in an airplane. In the book, however, it is Oddjob who gets sucked out of the plane window and not his boss; Goldfinger is strangled by Bond. This is apparently one of Ian Fleming's favorite methods for killing someone, because Blofeld also dies this way. And yes, the movie version of Oddjob's and Goldfinger's last few hours is definitely something much more spectacular.

In 1958, Gert Fröbe delivered such an impressive performance as a child murderer in the Swiss–West German film *Es geschah am hellichten Tag* (*It Happened in Broad Daylight*) that many moviegoers were afraid of him. That was exactly what the producers of the Bond movies also wanted. However, Fröbe was not the first choice for this job of playing Goldfinger; the fee wasn't high enough to tempt Orson Welles. Incidentally, Fröbe also played a role in another Fleming movie, *Chitty Chitty Bang Bang*, in 1968. At the same time that he was on the set in *Goldfinger*, he was also shooting *Those Magnificent Men in Their Flying Machines*.

Many passages of the movie have become legendary, especially thanks to Gert Fröbe's ingenious art of performance. This certainly includes the game of golf he plays with Bond, in which both cheat, but Bond does it more skillfully and leaves a furious Goldfinger behind. Or the scene in which Bond gets caught, leading to a classic exchange of words that will be repeated in many movies. The climax is essential 007: "Do you expect me to talk?" asks Bond, to which Goldfinger replies, "No, Mr. Bond! I expect you to die!" It is to Fröbe's credit that *Goldfinger* remains so popular today.

Gert Fröbe chatting with his colleague Terry-Thomas, with whom he acted in *Those Magnificent Men in Their Flying Machines.*
Image: Eric Koch / Anefo

Goldfinger's servant Oddjob shows Bond his hat—halfway between a bowler and a topper—with its razor-sharp brim. Later on, a deadly fight will unfold between the two. *Image: Picture Alliance*

Oddjob

One colorful character is Goldfinger's servant Oddjob, the man with the deadly but formal black hat. The scene in which he demonstrates his hat weapon and slices the head off a statue is one that will never be forgotten. Portraying Oddjob was Harold Sakata. Hailing from Hawaii, he had won a silver medal in weight lifting at the Olympic Games in 1948. He later worked as a professional wrestler. *Goldfinger* was his first movie role. Things could get rough when filming the fights; Sean Connery had to take a beating, and the contortions of pain on his face didn't require much acting.

Goldfinger's Rolls-Royce

Even Back Then, This Was a Classic Car

Before Goldfinger had to start "playing his golden harp," he had his servant Oddjob drive him around in a Rolls-Royce Phantom III. In the novel, Goldfinger owned an older, armored Rolls-Royce Silver Ghost—this model was manufactured between 1906 and 1926. This one had been made for a South American president, but he had been murdered before it was delivered. Rolls-Royce made the Phantom from 1925 to 1991, in several generations. In 2003, a new Phantom came on the market.

A Car Made of Gold

The car body of Goldfinger's Rolls-Royce is made of pure gold. This allows him to smuggle the precious metal across national borders. He later would have the Rolls disassembled and the gold melted down again, which was done in his factory in Switzerland. The increased weight of the car was apparently no problem when going through customs.

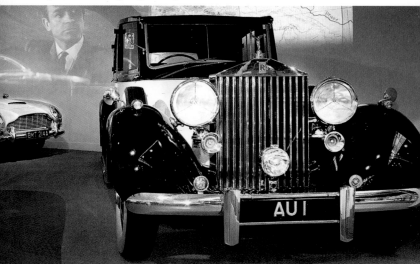

The chassis number on Goldfinger's Rolls-Royce was 3BU168. The two-tone body of this Sedanca de Ville was created by the Barker company. *Image: Newspress*

This profile image shows the elegant design of a 1937 Rolls-Royce Phantom III, with a car body made by Mulliner. *Image: Rolls-Royce Enthusiasts Club*

It was the Barker company that created the original design of the car body; Barker worked closely with Rolls-Royce. It stood for the conservative look. The vehicle was made for Lord Fairhaven. There were several other car body makers that gave this Rolls-Royce its look. Mulliner is one of the best known of them.

A Sedanca de Ville, also called a Coupe de Ville or town car, was a car in which the chauffeur sat outside or under an open top, but the passenger would be seated in a separate, closed part of the vehicle. This design is reminiscent of the carriages in earlier times. Goldfinger's license plate, "AU I," stands for his first name of Auric, but it is also the symbol for gold in the periodic table. The Roman numeral "I" goes without saying. However, it could also be an indication that the idea for this license plate may have been adopted from the *The Saint* TV series, which is discussed in chapters 11 and 38. In the show, the main character's license plate number was "ST I."

The Rolls-Royce Phantom III	
Production period:	1936–1939
Power output:	134 kW
Length:	213 inches (5,410 mm)
Height:	various
Width:	75 inches (1,905 mm)
Top speed:	87 mph (140 km/h)

Pussy's Flying Circus

The Bond Girls Phenomenon

34

Ian Fleming once confessed that the character of James Bond was born out of the angst of a newlywed husband who now had to largely give up his life as a sought-after single man. The "Bond girl" corresponded to classic male dreams, and that was certainly the reason it was such a successful ingredient in the 007 recipe.

At the same time, there is a range of Bond girl types. The female lead is generally a quite self-confident woman, who usually falls for Bond's charm—after showing a brief resistance—and comes to admire his superiority in the course of the plot. At the end of the novel version of *Goldfinger*, Ian Fleming characteristically writes of Pussy Galore: "She did as she was told, like an obedient child." Bond had tamed the proud woman.

Agent 007 often works with a colleague or a spy from another secret service. In Miranda Frost's case, however, this colleague is playing a deceptive game and is on the payroll of the main villain.

In the Roger Moore movies, especially, you often see entire hordes of lascivious female models, who were often enough played by beauty pageant winners. Being a Bond girl is a full-time job that goes well beyond making the movie. The ladies' schedules are filled up with press and photo appointments. A Bond girl would already be busy even before filming began, because the media wants photos and stories.

The Most Important Bond Girls

Movie	Actress
Dr. No	Honey Ryder (Ursula Andress)
	Sylvia Trench (Eunice Gayson)
	Miss Taro (Zena Marshall)
From Russia with Love	Tatiana Romanova (Daniela Bianchi)
	Sylvia Trench (Eunice Gayson)
Goldfinger	Jill Masterson (Shirley Eaton)
	Tilly Masterson (Tania Mallet)
	Pussy Galore (Honor Blackman)
Thunderball	Domino Derval (Claudine Auger)
	Fiona Volpe (Luciana Paluzzi)
	Patricia Fearing (Molly Peters)
You Only Live Twice	Helga Brandt (Karin Dor)
	Aki (Akiko Wakabayashi)
	Kissy Suzuki (Mie Hama)
On Her Majesty's Secret Service	Tracy di Vicenzo (Diana Rigg)
	Ruby Bartlett (Angela Scoular)
	Nancy (Catherine Schell)
Diamonds Are Forever	Tiffany Case (Jill St. John)
	Penny O'Toole (Lana Wood)
Live and Let Die	Solitaire (Jane Seymour)
	Rosie Carver (Gloria Hendry)
	Miss Caruso (Madeline Smith)
The Man with the Golden Gun	Andrea Anders (Maud Adams)
	Mary Goodnight (Britt Ekland)
The Spy Who Loved Me	Anya Amasova (Barbara Bach)
	Naomi (Caroline Munro)
Moonraker	Holly Goodhead (Lois Chiles)
	Corinne Dufour (Corinne Cléry)
	Manuela (Emily Bolton)
For Your Eyes Only	Melina Havelock (Carole Bouquet)
	Lisl von Schlaf (Cassandra Harris)
	Bibi Dahl (Lynn-Holly Johnson)
Never Say Never Again	Domino Petachi (Kim Basinger)
	Fatima Blush (Barbara Carrera)
Octopussy	Octopussy (Maud Adams)
	Magda (Kristina Wayborn)

The prototype of a Bond girl troop: Pussy Galore and her Flying Circus—the name was taken from Baron von Richthofen's fighter squadron during World War I. In the novel, however, Pussy Galore and her "Cement Mixers" were a gang of lesbian cat burglars. *Image: Danjaq/Newspress*

One thought-provoking story is that of the transgender Bond girl who acted in *For Your Eyes Only*. The "bathing beauty" Tula—which was the stage name of Caroline Cossey—at the villain Hector Gonzales's poolside hit the headlines after the movie was released. A tabloid owned by Rupert Murdoch, the role model for the villain Elliot Carver, revealed that she had undergone surgery. Of course, pictures of her with Roger Moore immediately circulated. For Tula, this was a catastrophe that led her to contemplate suicide. However, she resumed her modeling career and later released two autobiographies.

The Most Important Bond Girls

Movie	Actress
A View to a Kill	Stacey Sutton (Tanya Roberts)
	May Day (Grace Jones)
The Living Daylights	Kara Milovy (Maryam d'Abo)
License to Kill	Lupe Lamora (Talisa Soto)
	Pam Bouvier (Carey Lowell)
GoldenEye	Natalya Simonova (Izabella Scorupco)
	Xenia Onatopp (Famke Janssen)
Tomorrow Never Dies	Paris Carver (Teri Hatcher)
	Wai Lin (Michelle Yeoh)
The World Is Not Enough	Elektra King (Sophie Marceau)
	Dr. Christmas Jones (Denise Richards)
Die Another Day	Jinx Johnson (Halle Berry)
	Miranda Frost (Rosamund Pike)
Casino Royale	Vesper Lynd (Eva Green)
	Solange (Caterina Murino)
Quantum of Solace	Camille Montes Rivero (Olga Kurylenko)
	Strawberry Fields (Gemma Arterton)
Skyfall	Séverine (Bérénice Marlohe)
Spectre	Dr. Madeleine Swann (Léa Seydoux)
	Lucia Sciarra (Monica Bellucci)
	Estrella (Stephanie Sigman)
No Time to Die	Dr. Madeleine Swann (Léa Seydoux)
	Paloma (Ana de Armas)

Pussy Galore, played by Honor Blackman, is Auric Goldfinger's personal pilot and the leader of an all-woman flying squadron; she helps with Goldfinger's sinister plans. She seems immune to Bond's powers of seduction and appears to remain aloof. Here she is on the flight to Kentucky, to Goldfinger's big ranch, threatening the captured secret agent with a gun. Sean Connery appears to be a bit impressed. But he puts his trust in his charm and succeeds in bringing Pussy over to his side after an amorous tête-à-tête. Her lady pilots release some harmless clouds of fog instead of poison gas over the target, Fort Knox. As a result, the garrison manning the base survives and is able to repulse Goldfinger's troops. *Image: Danjaq/Newspress*

Falling for James Bond's Charms

The Ladies Who Get "Turned"

Roald Dahl (see page 108) once described the Bond girls' formula in *Playboy* magazine. The well-known author must certainly have known it well, because he wrote the script for *You Only Live Twice*. It should start out with a girl who is totally committed to 007. Unfortunately, her role includes the outcome that she will soon end up biting the dust. The best she can hope for is to be murdered in a very imaginative way—which will also cast the villain's horrible character in a very harsh light. The murder of Jill Masterson in *Goldfinger* is the textbook example of such a death, although she actually belongs to the second group: the Bond girl who starts out working for 007's antagonist. She is often even the antagonist's lover, and thanks to her skills she frequently causes Bond a lot of headaches. In any case, she is attracted by the secret agent's proverbial charm and excessive masculinity and ends up taking James Bond's side. The prototype is Pussy Galore.

A "Damascus Road" Conversion

Pussy Galore is a serious criminal who is working for Goldfinger and is even involved in the planning of his "Grand Slam" project, the attack on Fort Knox. Due to her conversion to the side of the good guys, she manages to thwart the villain's sinister plans. You will frequently find such ladies in a whole range of variations on a theme; they include Solitaire in *Live and Let Die*, Holly Goodhead in *Moonraker*, Octopussy in the movie of the same name, Kara in *The Living Daylights*, and finally Vesper Lynd in *Casino Royale*. Dahl also wants to see these ladies die, and that is what happens to ladies such as May Day in *A View to a Kill*, who ultimately comes over to Bond's side and allows herself to be sacrificed, or Fatima Blush in *Never Say Never Again*, who goes to bed with Bond only to show her own sexual prowess. And beyond these types, there is then the "good girl": characters such as Stacey Sutton in *A View to a Kill* or Christmas Jones in *The World Is Not Enough*.

The way Dahl typecasts these characters already contains a kernel of truth, but as always happens, when you catalog matters, you are simplifying them. And it is precisely these small differences that make the characters so interesting. Solitaire is attracted to 007; she fights back but doesn't stand a chance. Her flirtation with Bond causes her to lose her powers of second sight, and she is lost without them. This entire "cocktail" of ladies is just one big masculine wish fulfillment dream.

The Bond Girl Who Has to Die

In *Goldfinger,* Two Sisters at One Time

36

Jill and Tilly Masterson, two characters from the *Goldfinger* novel, also win honors in the movie. Jill dies what is perhaps the most famous death in movie history: after spending a night with James Bond, she is completely covered in gold paint and dies of asphyxiation for betraying Goldfinger. Her sister, Tilly, wants revenge and tries to gun Goldfinger down with a sniper rifle—which is, by the way, the same prop weapon that Ali Kerim Bey uses in *From Russia with Love* to shoot down the villain Krilencu. The weapon was part of the equipment in Bond's briefcase issued by Q's workshop. Tilly's attempt fails—and she ultimately has to atone for her failure by being executed by Oddjob's killer hat. She is one of those Bond girls who did not end up in bed with James Bond. The two sisters belong to a category of Bond girls who are there to be admired in many of the movies: pretty girls who become playmates of 007, but who have to pay for their affair with him (such as Jill) or their involvement in his mission in some way (such as Tilly) with their death.

Tania Mallet, the actress who played Tilly, was a sought-after model—like many of the other Bond girls who played smaller roles. After making this movie, she never wanted to work in the world of cinema again. As a rule, not many of the Bond girls have managed to use their role as a way to get their movie career off the ground. Many women who played the leading roles were also nowhere to be seen after their encounter with 007. Typical 007: the ladies may go, but Bond stays.

```
        E O N   P R O D U C T I O N S   L T D.


TO:    MR. WALLY EGGLEDEN
       c.c. Messrs. Saltzman
                    Broccoli
                    Sopel
       (For information: Mr. Guy Hamilton)

FROM:  L. C. RUDKIN          DATE:  6th January '64

-----------------------------------------------------

                "GOLDFINGER"
                -----------

Would you please make out a cheque payable to
British School of Motoring Ltd., value £17.12.6d.

I have arranged for Tania Mallett to take fifteen
driving lessons and the cheque will also cover
payment for her provisional driving licence and
test fee.
She is going to play the role of "Tilly".
```

EON takes care of everything. This document confirms that Tania Mallet (misspelled) took fifteen hours of driving lessons at the film studio's expense.
Image: ETH University Library Zurich, Picture Archive / Comet Photo AG (Zurich) / CC BY-SA 4.0

Tilly Masterson wants to avenge the spectacular death of her sister, Jill, who was coated entirely in gold paint by Oddjob. *Images: ETH Library Zurich, Image Archive / Comet Photo AG (Zurich) / CC BY-SA 4.0*

Bond drops Tilly off again at the Aurora gas station in the mountain village of Andermatt. He had given her a ride in his Aston Martin DB5 after his gadget had shredded her car's tires.

James Bond and Switzerland

A Return to His Mother's Homeland

Ian Fleming had already become so enthusiastic about the country during his first vacation in Switzerland as a sixteen-year-old that he not only studied there for a few years but also returned frequently. Therefore, it was certainly not by chance that several novels about secret agent 007 are set in this beautiful alpine country. Goldfinger, for example, has his factory in the environs of Geneva. *On Her Majesty's Secret Service* takes place mainly in Switzerland. To investigate clues about Ernst Stavro Blofeld, Bond travels to Bern to check out Blofeld's lawyer and visits Blofeld's mountaintop research clinic Piz Gloria.

Grandiose Shots and Sensational Ski Scenes

Bond's affinity for this country continued when they made the movies. The filmmakers took breathtaking shots there, especially in *Goldfinger* and in the George Lazenby movie (*On Her Majesty's Secret Service*). After the spectacular

A famous photo: Sean Connery as James Bond at the Furka Pass in Switzerland. According to Ian Fleming, Bond's mother was Swiss, so he is almost right at home. *Image: Aston Martin*

View from the Furka Pass during the filming of *Goldfinger*. Within a few moments, Bond will almost be hit by Tilly Masterson's shots at the villain. *Image: Aston Martin*

ski chase and the chase on the bobsled run in *On Her Majesty's Secret Service* were particularly well received, the idea was to repeat the same thing in other movies. Roger Moore went skiing in Switzerland in two of his movies.

An obituary for James Bond written by M for *The Times* newspaper when Bond has gone missing and is believed to be dead in *You Only Live Twice* reveals details of Bond's life. His father, Andrew Bond, came from the Scottish Highlands near the village of Glencoe, and his mother, Monique Delacroix, was from the Swiss canton of Vaud. When young James was just eleven years old, his parents were killed climbing in the Aiguilles Rouges mountains, near Chamonix, France. Thus, when James Bond travels to Switzerland, he is always visiting his mother's homeland again.

The Bond Car Par Excellence

Thanks to 007, the DB5 Became a Legend

38

Ian Fleming was a car buff, but automobiles didn't play as much of a role in his Bond novels as they did in the movies. The legendary car par excellence is the Aston Martin DB5. In *Goldfinger*, Q hands such a car over to 007 before he starts his mission. The filmmakers, first and foremost set designer Ken Adam, came up with a few features of equipment that turned a simple sports car into a true fighting machine. It is said that Adam thought up some of this equipment when he was sitting behind the wheel himself and getting annoyed with other drivers on the road, which is very easy to understand.

The abbreviation DB stands for David Brown of the David Brown Tractors Group in the United Kingdom, who owned Aston Martin for a long time. The tractor manufacturer thus fulfilled a dream—as Ferruccio Lamborghini did also. The number stands for the fifth model in the history of the sports car series under the aegis of David Brown. The Aston Martin DB5 could accelerate to

The Aston Martin DB5 with its *Goldfinger* license plate. This car has become more and more of an advertising icon in recent years. *Image: Aston Martin.*

The car body with its elegant Italian sports car–style curves was manufactured by Carrozzeria Touring Superleggera. Some 1,059 such cars were manufactured between 1963 and 1965.
Image: Aston Martin

62 mph (100 km/h) in 7.1 seconds. Its six-cylinder in-line engine with overhead camshafts was made of aluminum. The five-speed transmission was made by the ZF company in Friedrichshafen, Germany.

The Most Famous Used Car Ever

By the way, James Bond's car was secondhand. Q must have acquired it from the possession of Lord Yearley, otherwise known as actor Anthony Quayle. Thanks to the Saint, Simon Templar, Lord Yearly was arrested on TV on January 9, 1964, and no longer had any use for the car. His Aston Martin DB5 even kept its "BMT 216A" license plate—but also got another two besides (see page 80). The DB5 can be seen in the movies *Goldfinger*, *Thunderball*, *GoldenEye*, *Tomorrow Never Dies*, *The World Is Not Enough*, *Casino Royale*, *Skyfall*, *Spectre*, and *No Time to Die*.

In *Casino Royale*, Bond, alias Daniel Craig, wins an Aston Martin DB5 while gambling in the Bahamas, albeit one with left-hand drive.

The Aston Martin DB5

Production period:	1963–1965
Power output:	210 kW
Length:	180 inches (4,572 mm)
Height:	53 inches (1,346 mm)
Width:	66 inches (1,676 mm)
Top speed:	142 mph (229 km/h)

All the Gadgets on the DB5

The Secrets of 007's Company Car

39

Goldfinger marked a milestone for the 007 movie series. This movie was the first time that a whole range of technical shenanigans, called "**gadgets**," were used. The showpiece of Q's lab—which also produced Bond's diving suit with the fake seagull on the headgear, a bulletproof vest that had not been fully developed yet (fortunately, it had been developed sufficiently for the test subject to survive), and a parking meter that sprays tear gas—is undoubtedly the Aston Martin DB5, which has already been described in the previous chapter.

Briefing on His New Vehicle

James Bond gets a new car for his mission to spy on Goldfinger. His Bentley had been confiscated on M's instructions. What then follows has become a "golden oldie," because it is the first of the classic equipment

This image shows the device that is hidden under the car body of the DB5: a dummy machine gun that emerges from behind the turn signal. *Image: Aston Martin*

Three great gadgets on Bond's Aston Martin: a rotating license plate, retractable bumpers that function as battering rams, and built-in machine guns. *Image: Aston Martin*

handover exchanges between 007 and Q. Bond always acts as if he is a bit bored by Q's explanations and usually makes a few corny quips. The inventor is always annoyed by Bond's behavior and always angry about how negligently Bond treats the equipment. For many Bond fans, these verbal exchanges are an indispensable part of any genuine 007 movie.

But Now to the Gadgets!

In *Goldfinger*, the audience sees only the first part of the briefing on Bond's new company car. Q later explains that if Bond keeps paying attention, it all won't take more than an hour. In fact, there are some gadgets used later in the movie that the audience doesn't know about yet.

Q starts his presentation on the car by showing the bulletproof windows. That is nothing unusual so far, but something good to have if you are a secret agent. Also helpful are the two synchronously operating rotating license plates—valid for all countries, according to Q. In addition to the license number BMT 216A, registered in the United Kingdom, there is also a French number from the Département Pas-de-Calais, a region lying on the English Channel

Gadgets at the rear: retractable bumpers, rotating license plates, retractable bullet shields, blades in the wheels, and taillights that can be lowered and then spray out caltrops. *Image: Aston Martin*

Bond used these wheel blades to slash Tilly Masterson's tires. They bring back memories of *Ben Hur*. *Image: Dave McLear / CC BY 2.0*

opposite the English coast: 4711-EA-62. Besides this, the camera shows a license plate from Lucerne, Switzerland: LU 6789. However, 007 doesn't use it when in Switzerland; he stays with the real license number.

One very important gadget used in the movie is the Homer radar surveillance system (from "homing beacons"), which has a magnetic transmitter. Bond attaches it to Goldfinger's Rolls-Royce after their game of golf. The miniature receiver fits in the heel of his shoe, and the radar display with tracking screen is integrated into the dashboard. Q specifies that it has a range of up to 300 kilometers (186 miles).

Then Q displays the car's defense system in a console on the side. The front right lever activates a smoke generator through the exhaust pipes. The lever at the front left activates an oil sprayer behind the car's taillights. The brass switch at the rear raises the retractable bulletproof rear panel. The two MG 2 Browning machine guns, caliber 30, are operated from the middle; these are hidden behind the front turn signals. The final gadget is the button on the gearshift. It triggers the ejection seat on the passenger side. Bond makes fun of it all, saying, "Ejector seat? You're joking." But then Q utters his legendary and often-repeated remark: "I never joke about my work, 007!"

There are other gadgets that will be seen during the movie: retractable blades in the center locks on the wheels, a radio telephone, caltrops that fall out of the taillights and slash the tires of any pursuers, rams incorporated front and rear, and a lockable weapons compartment under the passenger seat. By the time the DB5 makes its second appearance in *Thunderball*, Q has installed a water cannon at the rear in addition to the old gadgets. Unfortunately, the car then went on an extended break until it returned to the screen in *GoldenEye*.

The car was equipped to spray slick oil on the road from the rear turn signal.
Image: Aston Martin

The Military and 007

Military Advisers, the Armed Forces, and Weapons

40

In the novel and movie versions of *Thunderball*, Bond has to deal with a military problem, something not unusual in his profession. A Royal Air Force aircraft carrying two H-bombs has gone missing. Blofeld's criminal organization Spectre is behind the deed. Emilio Largo is in charge of the operation, embodied quite impressively by Italian actor Adolfo Celi wearing an eye patch. This movie features a large number of underwater shots that eventually end up in a wild underwater battle.

Good Advice from Uncle Sam

When creating the movies, the filmmakers not only relied on Ian Fleming's descriptions and their own knowledge. When shooting *Thunderball*, they again hired the military adviser who had been part of the team since making

Colonel Russhon, here being treated to an ice cream cone by Sean Connery while filming *Thunderball*, was the movie team's military adviser for several years. *Image: Rachel Arroyo*

It was an RAF Avro Vulcan like this that Largo hijacked in *Thunderball*. It had two H-bombs on board, which he wanted to use for terror attacks. *Image: Sgt. David S. Nolan, US Air Force*

From Russia with Love. Charles J. Russhon was a US Air Force colonel with experience making movies, and he had ties too with England, because he had served in the British theater of war in Burma during World War II and was even awarded a medal. He was the first photographer allowed to visit the destroyed city of Hiroshima. Russhon was able to use his connections to pull strings, which worked out well when the crew was allowed to film at Fort Knox—although not inside, since no one is allowed to do that. He made a cameo appearance in *Thunderball* as an Air Force officer. In *Goldfinger*, his name appears in the credits, and he even gets promoted, because the barracks at Fort Knox were named after one General Russhon. Russhon, a native New Yorker, also managed to get the streets needed to film the car chase in *Live and Let Die* blocked off—no small feat in the notoriously congested Big Apple. He was known for his love of ice cream, which explains the backstory for the photo at left showing Sean Connery feeding the colonel an ice cream cone. Bond was issued a whole range of **gadgets** for his mission, such as a pill that transmits his location, a small oxygen cartridge for diving, and an infrared underwater camera.

The Flying Bond

An Early Highlight in *Thunderball*

The opening sequence of a James Bond movie often depicts a short and crisp mission just by itself, which usually has nothing to do with the main plot. In *Thunderball*, Bond has the task of neutralizing the enemy agent Jacques Bouvar. He has dressed himself up as a widow and comes home from his own funeral. 007 is able to eliminate Bouvar after a

short fight. To escape, Bond uses a rocket backpack, which, incidentally, had been organized by Colonel Russhon (see chapter 40). This gadget makes another appearance in the twentieth Bond movie, when Pierce Brosnan finds it in Q's workshop and asks if it's still in working order. James Bond is able land right next to his DB5 and flee.

Shooting the opening sequence of *Thunderball*. Bond uses a rocket backpack to escape from the château after he killed his antagonist, Colonel Jacques Bouvar. At left in the foreground is his Aston Martin.
Bouvar is played by stuntman and Bond double Bob Simmons.
Image: Danjaq/Newspress

Bond Day and the Headlines

Media Hype about James Bond, Agent 007

42

Since the first time Sean Connery announced that he by no means ever wanted to play James Bond again, media speculation about who would be the "new Bond" has gone out of control. This has become a real sport over the years. In addition, media speculation is a way for interested actors to get their names into the discussions. Sean Connery announced his first resignation in the *Los Angeles Times* before the filming of *You Only Live Twice* had even been completed. This time he was serious. Because George Lazenby's performance didn't convince the studio, they gave Connery a golden handshake to return in *Diamonds Are Forever*. And then he came back for seconds.

The Second Resignation from His Resignation

The phrase "Never say never again" is often attributed to Sean Connery declaring he would never play Bond again—and then doing it again. However, it is a citation from Ian Fleming himself and comes from his children's book *Chitty Chitty Bang Bang*: "That's no way to treat adventures. Never say no to adventures. Always say yes. Otherwise, you'll lead a very dull life."

The movie *Never Say Never Again* is actually a remake of *Thunderball*. It is not counted as part of the official Bond movie franchise, although a former 007 was on board. The opening sequence and the Bond "anthem" had to be dispensed with, but not the participation of top-class stars, including Max von Sydow, Edward Fox, Kim Basinger, and Klaus Maria Brandauer. The racy Barbara Carrera, whose name was already synonymous with successful car chases, was part of the package. In addition, Rowan Atkinson, the future Mr. Bean, made an appearance in a supporting role. This brilliant actor had just made his breakthrough into the top ranks of British comedians in 1983 with *Blackadder*. In 2003, he fulfilled his dream of playing the role of a Bond-like secret agent himself in the James Bond parody *Johnny English*. Incidentally, like James Bond, he's a real car fanatic. In *Never Say Never Again*, he plays the embassy clerk Nigel Small-Fawcett in the Bahamas. In the novel *Casino Royale*, one of Bond's assistants in Jamaica is called Fawcett.

This time around, Largo's ship is called the *Flying Saucer*. It belonged to a friend of Sean Connery's who made it available for filming. Ultimately, there is no game of cards or dice. This time, Bond and his enemy Largo compete in an ultramodern computer game that Largo had programmed himself. In his contract,

James Bond Day is always duly celebrated by the car manufacturer Aston Martin. Here is a decorated display window in one of the company's car dealerships. *Image: Aston Martin*

Sean Connery was given an enormous say in the production. He was also allowed to suggest the casting of the most important actors. This is how it came out that he was a *Playboy* reader, because he had proposed casting Barbara Carrera after reading this trade journal for "men's issues." His lovely wife is said not to have appreciated this at all. She demonstratively visited the set when there was shooting involving Ms. Carrera and her husband. She need not have worried, because their relationship was far too explosive . . .

For movie fans all over the world, *Never Say Never Again* versus *Octopussy* was the greatest duel in movie history. Connery versus Moore. Who is the "real" Bond? It was a feast for the media; 007 was the hottest movie topic in the press and would remain so. Who is better? When is the next movie coming out? What is it called? Who is the Bond girl? Who is the bad guy? And who will be the new Bond? Issues that move the world. In the past, the thirst for Bond-related secrets has even spurred people to hack into the production company to uncover internal information. Bond is increasingly becoming a hallmark of excellence; anytime he is to be found standing next to a product, it can only mean that this is "the best." One special feature that probably no other novel or movie hero can boast of is Global James Bond Day. It has been celebrated on October 5 since 2012. The occasion for this tradition's inception was the fiftieth anniversary of the premiere of the first Bond movie, *Dr. No*, in London. Anyone celebrating the day properly has to drink a martini, and many companies and cultural institutions take part. In 2012, by the way, Adele's Bond song "Skyfall" was published punctually at 0:07 a.m.

The Ravages of Time

Sean Connery and His Toupee

43

For Connery, *Never Say Never Again* was certainly a very successful interpretation of the Bond character, even if he appears to be a bit stiff when dancing with Domino. He'll get it all out later on in the showdown with Fatima. In the run-up to the movie, there were countless comments in the media about his age. That had not happened to Roger Moore in 1983, even though he had been born two years earlier than the Scotsman.

Despite this late appearance after a twelve-year hiatus, Sean Connery is not the oldest Bond in movie history. In fact, Roger Moore was fifty-seven years old when he made his last movie, and David Niven was the same age in 1967's *Casino Royale*.

Sean Connery was already wearing a toupee on his head during the filming of *Goldfinger*. In the picture at left, you can see him shortly after the completion of *Never Say Never Again* without any makeup and with the mustache he was wearing at the time. At a press conference following *You Only Live Twice*, when he was annoyed by all the press hype, he appeared without his toupee, which apparently caused a shock among some.

Connery often showed off his hairy chest in the movies—a sign of masculinity at the time. Things are very different with Daniel Craig. He presents his body clean-shaven, in keeping with the taste of the times.

Sean Connery without makeup in the year of *Never Say Never Again*. The French actress Saskia Cohen-Tanugi, who played his colleague Nicole in the movie, is at his side at right in the picture. *Image: Rob Bogaerts / Anefo*

The Spy Who Loved Me
The Novel Has Nothing to Do with the Movie

This book was an interesting experiment. Unlike the rest of the James Bond novels, 007 is not the main character. Rather, he appears only late in the book as the rescuing angel. The young Canadian Vivienne Michel is the narrator of the story. She was left an orphan when she was eight; her parents were killed in a plane crash. Her aunt raised her and sent her to England for her education. There, she started having some affairs. She was being prosecuted by the police for a sexual encounter with a lover in a movie theater. Another lover, a German from the city of Augsburg, got her pregnant. In her desperate situation, she had an abortion and then left England to travel through eastern North America on a Vespa scooter. She takes a job at the reception desk in a motel to finance her continued journey. Now things get creepy. Two criminals force their way in and hold her prisoner. By chance, James Bond is passing by; he kills the villains and leaves Vivienne after an amorous tête-à-tête.

When his books were being made into movies, Ian Fleming forbade anyone from putting this novel on the big screen. However, the title of the novel was released by his heirs. This was because it has a good ring to it and promises the two most important ingredients of a Bond story: spies and love. A movie of the same name was made in 1977, but it is an entirely different matter than the book. You see Bond skiing, with killers in pursuit. He saves himself by jumping into the abyss, which was a record-breaking stunt. Two submarines, one Soviet and one British, are hijacked. Bond is supposed to investigate the matter and has a wild adventure dealing with the villain Karl Stromberg.

An Ingenious Sports Car

Bond's New Car Was Also a Submarine

In the novel *The Spy Who Loved Me*, the two diabolical villains end up driving their car into a lake and drowning. Presumably that was the trigger for the scriptwriters to come up with a story line about a vehicle underwater. Of course, since it was Bond's company car, such a plunge into the water would have to end in glory. The car was a Lotus Esprit S3.

An Automotive Legend Made in England

Lotus Cars has its headquarters in a small town in eastern England. The company was founded by the design engineer Colin Chapman. He became known to sports fans as the head of the Lotus Formula I racing team. After all, his team produced five world champion drivers: Jim Clark (who even won twice), Graham Hill, Jochen Rindt, Emerson Fittipaldi, and Mario Andretti. Truly illustrious names! The team has even won the World Constructors Championship seven times. Lotus is known for its exquisite sports cars. The Esprit model is the one that has been part of this car manufacturer's range the longest. Over time, however, new

Roger Moore, alias James Bond, is given a white Lotus Esprit by Q in *The Spy Who Loved Me*. It boasts of all sorts of little extras. *Image: Collection of Michael Dörflinger*

versions of the model have made their appearance. The first Lotus Esprit was presented to the public as early as 1972. But it took another four years before the first customer was able to get delivery of his car. The second generation of cars began to roll out of the workshop in 1978; two years later, the third series, the Esprit S3, appeared.

Special Equipment from the Q Branch

The engine of the Esprit S1 generated 162 hp and was able to accelerate the 1,984-pound (900-kilogram) vehicle to 135 mph (217 km/h). However, the vehicle that Q worked on probably weighed a lot more than the standard model, because he equipped it with some of the most spectacular **gadgets** that 007 was ever allowed to put into action. Bond's company car could be transformed into a submarine at the push of a button. It also featured onboard missiles. From under the water, Bond manages to shoot down the helicopter of his pursuer Naomi with a missile. The underwater scenes were filmed not just in the Bahamas but also at Pinewood Studios near London. They built a huge hall there, which was named the "007 Stage."

The striking wedge shape of the Lotus Esprit S1 shows the characteristic thumbprint of the Italian star designer Giorgetto Giugiaro of the Italdesign company. *Image: Lotus*

This legendary scene was filmed in Sardinia. After a gripping underwater dive, Bond emerges from the water in his Lotus, leaving the swimmers on the shore flabbergasted. *Image: Lotus/Newspress*

During the underwater chase, Bond indulges in a joke, which is what makes the Roger Moore movies so special. Before making a turn, he switches on the turn signal, which indicates one direction—but then he turns the other way. He tops that when he drives out of the water. The stunned beachgoers are even more surprised when 007 tosses a fish out of his car. Besides all this, the car can also spray dirt onto the windshield of a pursuer's car.

Of course, the Esprit wasn't Bond's only **gadget**. In the opening sequence, he uses a ski pole to shoot. He has a cigarette case with a small x-ray machine that allows him to open safes. He also drives a collapsible personal watercraft (prototype from the Spirit Marine company) and is issued a microfilm reader that is contained in an eyeglass case. Unfortunately, he is not allowed to take the shooting shisha water pipe or the murderous camel saddle from Q's laboratory along with him.

The Lotus Esprit S1

Production period:	1976–1978
Power output:	119 kW
Length:	165 inches (4,191 mm)
Height:	43.75 inches (1,111 mm)
Width:	73.3 inches (1,861 mm)
Top speed:	135 mph (217 km/h)

An Antagonist with a Bite

One of 007's Best-Known Enemies

Besides Blofeld and Goldfinger, there is probably no other Bond villain who has remained so well remembered as Jaws. He emerges on the screen for the first time in *The Spy Who Loved Me* and makes a second appearance in *Moonraker*. In the latter movie, he cleans up his act thanks to his new girlfriend and finally uses his Herculean strength to bail Bond out of a tight spot.

A Nightmare for Any Secret Agent.

Jaws is a really big guy who parts his hair in the middle. He gets his name from his set of metal teeth, which he can even use to bite apart thick cable car cables. The model for Jaws is the killer "Horror" Horowitz from the novel *The Spy Who Loved Me*. This sinister figure has dental crowns made of steel, but he cannot use them the way Jaws can. By the way, Horowitz doesn't smoke, something that Bond doesn't like at all: "It's only pros that don't." "Horror" also has a completely bald colleague, the role model for Sandor, who appears only briefly in the movie. He had already departed this life during the first encounter in Cairo. Both work for Karl Stromberg.

Despite his somewhat dim-witted appearance, Jaws is actually quite clever and knows how to plan his actions. When Stromberg declares open hunting season on James Bond, the epic pursuit of 007 is launched on land, in the sea, and in the air. Jaws takes part in this campaign. He should have died in the end, but given the excitement about this character, Jaws was allowed to survive and once again plays a part in

A happy ending for Jaws: In Rio de Janeiro, he meets little Dolly with her kiddie-style pigtails. She makes the archvillain clean up his act.
Image: Danjaq/Newspress

Jaws and his accomplice on the hunt for 007 and his Lotus. But they had bad luck: their pursuit ends in the dwelling of a wine-drinking senior. *Image: Danjaq/Newspress*

Moonraker. In this movie, something really annoying happens: his parachute doesn't open, but he manages to land safely on a circus big top.

During the Carnival celebrations in Rio, Jaws tries to murder Bond's partner, Manuela, on a side street. Fortunately, other Carnivalists, who apparently think he is just another masked reveler, drag him along to celebrate with them. Later, there is a dramatic three-way battle among him, Bond, and Holly Goodhead on the cable car. Once again, things turn out badly for Jaws, but when he crashes at full speed into the valley station in his gondola and it all collapses, he meets Dolly. The little miss with her saucy pigtails is still unable to prevent Jaws from continuing to pounce on Bond. This time he chases Bond down a Brazilian river—and goes plunging over the Iguazú Falls. Ultimately, however, little Dolly's good influence leads Jaws to save the lives of Holly and Bond.

Jaws was also able to cause pain just by being there: the director of the two movies, Lewis Gilbert, suffered from neck pain after a few days of shooting—because he always had to look up at Jaws actor Richard Kiel. For Kiel, it was the role of his life, and years later he continued to showcase himself as part of the 007 movie franchise.

The Antagonist Is Stronger

A Common Theme in Bond Movies

47

Jaws was certainly the most spectacular representative of a certain type of character in the Bond movies, but there have been many others like him over the years. Here we're talking about the incredibly strong giant who doesn't seem to mind Bond's blows—the enemy who is the stronger one. This lovely species seems to be indestructible on God's green earth—and in the air. These characters often have special and imaginatively devised weapons: a set of steel teeth, a metal prosthetic arm like Tee Hee has, or a bowler hat with a razor-sharp edge. Once it is even a woman of Herculean strength: the extravagant May Day. Her name says it all.

Real Fighting Machines

These sinister characters usually serve as the executors for the leading villain. In their battles with James Bond, they have the upper hand, and it seems like it is only a matter of time before 007 will have to give up the ghost. But then Bond reaches into his bag of tricks. An example of this scenario occurs in Luxor, Egypt, where Bond seems to have no chance against Jaws, since his blows make no impact at all. Bond is able to triumph only by managing to use a beam to dodge a blow from his antagonist, so that Jaws ends up hitting a wooden pillar of the scaffolding, causing everything above him to collapse.

Hinx, the beefy accomplice in *Spectre*, is considered the outstanding antagonist of this category in the Daniel Craig movies. His brutal appearance at the meeting of Blofeld's criminal organization is already a memorable introduction. He is the only one keeping track of things in the hustle and bustle after Bond is unmasked, and he chases 007 in a Jaguar C-X75 in a mad car race through Rome and along the quay of the Tiber River. Later he kidnaps Madeleine Swann from the mountain clinic. It appears that he has already been eliminated after a breathtaking chase (see page 176), but no: he returns to the screen and engages Bond in a wild scuffle in an Oriental Desert Express railroad car in Morocco. But he fails, like some other villains have done before him: by his cleverness, Bond succeeds in throwing Hinx off the train.

How these pictures look alike: Dave Bautista shooting out of a car in *Spectre*. He is one of Bond's seemingly overwhelming enemies, who can ultimately be defeated only by the secret agent's resourcefulness. *Image: Newspress*

Lazenby, the Male Model

From a Beacon of Hope to a Flash in the Pan

Today, *On Her Majesty's Secret Service* is considered one of the most interesting and best Bond movies. Compared to many of the other movie adaptations of the novels, this flick sticks very closely to the original. However, very few people really warmed to the new actor playing James Bond. George Lazenby was generally considered to be miscast. At the time, there was a rumor circulating that this appearance wasn't the first time Lazenby played Bond, because he had been the stuntman for Sean Connery, nine years his senior. But that's wrong. The Australian made his home in London at the time and worked as a male model. As an actor, he had no previous experience, apart from making commercials. Nevertheless, he got the role, certainly primarily thanks to his vague resemblance to Sean Connery, which Lazenby emphasized during the casting by wearing a suit typical of the Scotsman.

The Footprints Were Too Big for Him

There was one funny touch in the scene after Tracy's suicide attempt and the robbery: Lazenby's line "This never happened to the other fellow." He was referring to Sean Connery. In reality, however, he also had enough scenes in which he drew the short straw. The final scene with the dead Tracy in his arms had to be done again because Lazenby had tears in his eyes. But that did not please the director. Lazenby's other ideas, such as giving Bond in a hippie look, with long hair and a full beard, were also rejected.

Lazenby is the only Bond to be seen in his own office at MI6 and the only one who gives Moneypenny a kiss on the mouth (Pierce Brosnan's kiss wasn't real because Moneypenny had borrowed Q's virtual-reality glasses).

He makes a rather wooden impression: George Lazenby as James Bond. *Image: Collection of M. Dörflinger*

He was elegantly dressed and had the cool smoking style of a Humphrey Bogart, but Lazenby did not go down particularly well with audiences. *Image: ETH University Library Zurich, Picture Archive / Comet Photo AG (Zurich) / CC BY-SA 4.0*

Winter Sports in the Movies

James Bond Goes Skiing and Bobsledding

49

Ernst Stavro Blofeld's institute is located on the fictional Piz Gloria, which actually is the Schilthorn, a summit in the Bernese Alps in Switzerland. So it stands to reason that people also ski in the area. That created an opportunity for Willy Bogner, the former German World Championship skier. With this movie, he was responsible for the ski scenes in a Bond flick for the first time, and he also took care of the spectacular camera shots. As he did so, he would go plunging down the mountain with his camera in hand. An incredible achievement when you consider that this equipment was significantly larger and heavier than today's helmet cameras. Besides this, he also often skied backward; to do this, he used trick skis that were bent upward at the tip and the tail.

The ski chase went down really well with the fans. As a result, in subsequent movies, filmmakers would always have some part of the plot play out in the mountains. Bogner also filmed in *The Spy Who Loved Me* and *For Your Eyes Only*, and he directed the ski scenes in *A View to a Kill*. Of course, there are also gadgets available on the slopes. Thus, in *The Spy Who Loved Me*, Bond's ski pole is also a rifle. The villains in *The World Is Not Enough* pursue Bond and Elektra in paraglider snowmobiles.

Among the team working on *On Her Majesty's Secret Service* was Bernhard Russi, a young Swiss skier who was at the beginning of a great career. In 1972, he won Olympic gold in the downhill event in Sapporo, Japan. But things might have turned out differently, because when filming the Bond movie in early 1969, he had a bad fall during the ski chase from the Schilthorn summit down to the valley. He broke a cervical vertebra, and it was only at the end of the year that he was able to take part in a world championship race again. Today, he and his company design downhill tracks for major events. His ties to Willy Bogner have remained firm. The latter is, in fact, the head of the Swiss branch of Russi's company and sits on the board of directors.

Down the Track at Hellish Speed

Bobsledding is another discipline that lends itself to wild pursuits. *On Her Majesty's Secret Service* also features this winter sport, in the sequence when 007 followed Blofeld, who was fleeing in a bobsled, down the icy track on skis. Another bobsled sequence was filmed for *For Your Eyes Only*. Most unfortunately, it involved a fatal accident. When the bobsled ran off the track, the stuntman at the rear was killed.

View from Piz Gloria, where Blofeld resided. It was from this summit that James Bond skied down into the valley, with Blofeld's henchmen on his tail. *Image: ETH University Library Zurich, Picture Archive / Comet Photo AG (Zurich) / CC BY-SA4.0*

Willy Bogner filming on skis with Roger Moore. *Image: Picture Alliance*

Blofeld: Bond's Intimate Enemy

The Man of a Thousand Faces

In the beginning, Ernst Stavro Blofeld was a man without a face. What you primarily saw was a white cat lolling comfortably in the villain's lap. It was not until *You Only Live Twice* that the audience got to see what he looked like: completely bald, a staring gaze, and a scar across his blinded right eye. The bald head stayed, but otherwise Telly Savalas did not dress up much. As Gert Fröbe did when playing Goldfinger, Savalas almost upstaged his counterpart, James Bond. Blofeld is the head of the worldwide criminal organization Spectre. In *On Her Majesty's Secret Service*, Blofeld stated that his ancestors came from the city of Augsburg in Germany and that he wanted to secure the title of Count von Bleuchamp for himself. Ultimately, it is this vanity that brings him down. But he just will not die, even if Sean Connery drowns him or Roger Moore throws him down a chimney. After all, following *Never Say Never Again*, he spends thirty-two years in the wilderness, in order to then reappear once again.

Blofeld in the 007 Franchise

Movie	Actor
From Russia with Love	Anthony Dawson
Thunderball	Anthony Dawson
You Only Live Twice	Donald Pleasence
On Her Majesty's Secret Service	Telly Savalas
Diamonds Are Forever	Charles Gray
For Your Eyes Only	John Hollis
Never Say Never Again	Max von Sydow
Spectre	Christoph Waltz
No Time to Die	Christoph Waltz

Blofeld—Almost Related to James Bond

The movie *Spectre* shows a new aspect of Blofeld. This time, the villain, played by Christoph Waltz, gleefully reveals that he is actually Franz Oberhauser, the foster brother of James Bond, and that as Blofeld he is behind all the setbacks that 007 encounters. Yet, his attempt at murder fails, and in the end he is arrested by the London police after a furious showdown. In the short story "Octopussy," one Hannes Oberhauser appeared as a ski instructor and mountain guide in Kitzbühel in the Austrian Alps. He had been murdered by Dexter Smythe shortly after World War II. For the James Bond in the story, he was a father figure who had taught Bond to ski.

Telly Savalas was one of the most fascinating actor antagonists of the British agent with the license to kill. *Image: ETH University Library Zurich, Picture Archive / Comet Photo AG (Zurich) / CC BY-SA 4.0*

Bond's marriage to the fiery Tracy was brought to an end on the very same day as the wedding by Blofeld and Irma Bunt.

Image: ETH University Library Zurich, Picture Archive / Comet Photo AG (Zurich) / CC BY-SA 4.0

James Bond's Marriages

51

The Unforgettable Tracy— and What of Madeleine?

She had finally done it: in *On Her Majesty's Secret Service*, Tracy di Vicenzo has captured the volatile heart of the British agent and even got him to hang up his professional hat. That goes for the novel as well as for the movie. Diana Rigg, who had already enchanted the men of the 1960s as a self-confident beauty in *The Avengers*, played the strife-torn Tracy brilliantly as she wavered between suicide and hauteur. Her father, Draco, is an underworld boss, but he helps 007 in the search for Blofeld and allies himself with Bond. He wants Bond to take care of Tracy, which 007 does at first reluctantly and then more and more enthusiastically. On the run from Blofeld, Tracy and Bond get caught in an avalanche. Tracy is captured, but Bond, Draco, and his men are able to free her. Is there a happy ending? The two get married. But their happily ever after is short lived because, with Irma Bunt pulling the trigger and Blofeld at the wheel, the villains fire shots at the honeymooners' car. Tracy dies. Bond's marriage is over in just one day.

Tracy is also killed in the novel. There, however, these scenes take place in Bavaria. They get married at the British consulate in Munich and then travel on the A 8 Autobahn superhighway and then along the Inntal (Inn Valley) Autobahn in Austria toward Kitzbühel. Shortly after they pass the exit for the German city of Rosenheim, shots are fired from a black Mercedes. This time it was Blofeld himself who had pulled the trigger.

In *You Only Live Twice*, 007 enters into a fictitious marriage with Kissy Suzuki in order to fulfill his mission. And then there is Dr. Madeleine Swann. The blond beauty from *Spectre* manages to get Bond to quit his work. In an impressive final scene, he must decide whether to exact his revenge on Blofeld or win over Madeleine. He decides that she will be his choice. In *No Time to Die*, they start the movie as a couple, but villainous forces conspire to tear them apart.

The villain Hinx kidnaps Ms. Swann. But Bond gives it everything he has to win her over.
Image: Newspress

James Bond at Work in Japan

On the Hunt for His Archenemy

52

The English versions of the novel and movie for *You Only Live Twice* are similar in terms of plot. The movie adopts many passages from Ian Fleming, but the misdeeds committed by primary villain Blofeld are totally different, and many of the action scenes were invented by the scriptwriters.

The False Death

The title of the book reflects a haiku that James Bond wrote during his training in all things Japanese: "You only live twice: once when you are born, and once when you are looking death in the face." This is taken very literally in the movie because a gang of the villains attacks Bond after he has engaged in an amorous tête-à-tête, and apparently they kill him. At least that's what the newspapers report. This trick allows 007 to go underground and work undisturbed. This all involves a chase and some ingenious action when a helicopter carrying a big magnet catches a car, pulls it up, and lets it fall again once over the sea.

Tiger Tanaka, the Japanese counterpart to M, provides Bond with some express training in being Japanese and for working as a secret-service agent at

Portrait of Roald Dahl on a Norwegian airplane. Image: Adam Moreira (AEMoreira042281) / CC4.0

Screenwriter Roald Dahl, a Commander in H. M. Secret Service

The screenplay for *You Only Live Twice* was written by British author Roald Dahl. A year later, he wrote the screenplay for *Chitty Chitty Bang Bang*, another time an Ian Fleming novel was made into a movie. Dahl certainly knew what he was writing about, because he had served as a pilot in World War II, but then he switched to the Secret Intelligence Service. In the United States, Dahl worked—as James Bond did— as an agent for the British secret service,

and it was here that he worked with Ian Fleming. He later wrote children's books and some humorous, macabre prose.

In the movie, Himeji Castle served as the Japanese secret police headquarters. This is where James Bond learned the martial arts practiced by the ninja warriors. *Image: yokoyokoi / CC BY-SA 3.0*

the ninja training school for East Asian martial arts. Agent 007 is also "Japanized" in terms of his looks; unfortunately, the makeup artists achieved only fragmentary success in doing this. Then the intention is to have him penetrate Blofeld's fortified headquarters in the crater of a volcano. In the novel, this is actually a castle built on a steep rock face.

Not a Pretty Way to Die

In the novel, Bond—like Sean Connery in the film—is trapped by a trapdoor, and his antagonists want to kill him using an apparatus that is either a kind of toilet or an altar, by a hot jet from the ground driven into his posterior. But the novel's Bond is able to free himself and strangles Blofeld with his bare hands, which is what he had done previously to Goldfinger. His escape in a balloon is not completely successful because he falls from a great height into the sea and loses his memory. As a result, he ends up living for several years as the simple fisherman Taro Todoroki with his pretend wife, Kissy Suzuki. The movie James Bond, on the other hand, is able not only to destroy Blofeld's structure but also to prevent World War III. Yet, the movie's Blofeld managed to escape in a mini submarine.

Bond Raises Toyota to the Peerage

His Sports Car Was Actually a Yamaha

53

There was a time when many Japanese cars still looked like loose copies of the European classics. The similarity of the Toyota 2000 GT to the Jaguar E-Type just cannot be denied. Only 351 of these cars were ever made, plus the two as a convertible model for the James Bond movie *You Only Live Twice*. The six-cylinder in-line engine with an engine displacement of 2 liters had a power output of 110 kW. Thus, you could drive the 2000 GT at speeds of up to 137 mph.

The Visions of a Motorcycle Manufacturer

In 1959, Yamaha established a research-and-development department to design its own Japanese sports car. It very soon became clear that the requirements for launching the car on the market were beyond the group's capabilities. Therefore, they sought contact with established car manufacturers so they could enter a cooperative relationship with them.

Because Nissan had dropped out, Yamaha turned to Toyota. At the time, this company was considered very conservative and manufactured family cars suitable for the general public. But things worked out. However, Toyota refashioned the design for the 2000 GT. The car was designed with a central tube frame, on which the aluminum car body was built. The cars were assembled by Yamaha but sold under the Toyota brand. Due to its high price, the car was certainly not intended for the mass market.

The Toyota 2000 GT convertible model was manufactured to specifications and made only for the Bond movie *You Only Live Twice*. The car belonged to the pretty Japanese secret agent Suki.
Image: Newspress

The in-line six-cylinder engine with two overhead camshafts made it possible for this chic Toyota sports car to achieve some great racing successes and world records. *Image: Toyota*

The head of Toyota managed to convince movie director Lewis Gilbert that only a local model of car should be considered for filming in Japan. It was the ideal opportunity for him to showcase the new 2000 GT, which had come out a month before the premiere of the new Bond movie. But then there was a problem!

Sean Connery Was Too Tall to Get in the Car

At a height of 6 feet, 2 inches, Sean Connery did not fit into the low car, which itself had a height of less than 4 feet. Therefore, two of the vehicles were very rapidly transformed into convertibles. Thanks to the central tube frame construction, it was possible to do this without creating any difficulties with the statics. The convertible top was just a dummy, however. It remained on just those two individual cars, because the Japanese were not introducing any roadsters into their model range. Incidentally, the Toyota 2000 GT is Daniel Craig's favorite Bond car.

The Toyota 2000 GT	
Production period:	1967–1970
Power output:	112 kW
Length:	164.4 inches (4,175 mm)
Height:	46 inches (1,170 mm)
Width:	63 inches (1,600 mm)
Top speed:	137 mph (220 km/h)

Little Nellie Has It Her Way

Bond Scores Four Aerial Victories in a Mini Helicopter

54

Q is also in Japan, and unlike the younger Q featured in the movies from *Skyfall* onward, he does not suffer from a fear of flying. He is bringing along a fabulous souvenir in his four suitcases: the miniature helicopter named "Little Nellie," which anyone can just screw together by themselves. This model was a Wallis WA-116 Agile Series 1, and in the movie the man who made it, Ken Wallis, flew it himself. The aircraft, weighing only about 254 pounds (115 kilograms), managed a top speed of 129 mph (208 km/h) and had a total range of just under 7 miles (11 kilometers). Something ideal for making a reconnaissance flight over the island, where one suspects Blofeld has his headquarters.

But James Bond does not go unnoticed. Four Bell 47 G-3 helicopters attack him from behind. An exciting aerial battle begins. Thanks to his various onboard **gadgets**, 007 is able to deal with his antagonists, using machine guns, rocket launchers, flamethrowers, smoke machines, and aerial mines. However, there was also one genuine casualty during the shoot: when filming a shot of a helicopter from above, cameraman John Jordan was struck by a rotor blade and lost one of his feet.

Brought together in the National Motor Museum in Beaulieu, UK: Little Nellie is in front of the tuk-tuk taxi from *Octopussy* on the left, with the BMW 750iL from *Tomorrow Never Dies* in the background. *Image: Newspress*

Rumors about Shatterhand

This Name Comes Up Time and Again

A James Bond movie always arouses interest in the objects, areas, or customs it features. More and more, businesses have taken advantage of this phenomenon and have presented their products in an artful way. But the 007 fan base also discovers other interesting things (see pages 120 or 152, for example). One surprising consequence of the flick set in Japan was a veritable ninja craze, although it was the Western ninja movies that really cashed in, especially during the 1980s.

Shatterhand Just Can't Be a Bad Guy

In Germany, many people were bemused when they heard that the working title for the twenty-fifth Bond movie was *Shatterhand*, because Shatterhand is the name of the splendid hero of the travel stories by nineteenth-century German author Karl May. "Old Shatterhand" is a German American who helps pacify the Wild West with his very special weapons and who—with his blood brother, the Native American Winnetou—ensures that the good side wins! How could he appear in a Bond movie?

It is precisely because this name was so famous in Germany that the translator had to intervene when the novel *You Only Live Twice* was translated into German. In the original novel, Dr. Guntram Shatterhand is the false name that Blofeld assumes when he appears in Japan as a kind of guru for the candidates for suicide missions. That simply would not do in Germany, especially at a time when there still was real "Karl May fever." The name was simply changed to Guntram Martell without further ado. The new name also works in German, because there is not so much difference between a hammer ("Martell" is an old Frankish word for hammer) and a "Shatter hand" ("Schmetterhand" in German).

Fleming is said to have taken the name of "Shatterhand" from a cafe that he had once visited in Hamburg, Germany. By the way, Old Shatterhand really was an antagonist of 007—at the box office. In 1962, the German movie *Der Schatz im Silberse* (*The Treasure in Silver Lake*) hit the silver screen, and it topped the number of ticket sales for *Dr. No* in Germany. But it was all soon over for such movies, which were very loosely based on Karl May's works, while the adventures of British secret agent 007 today remain among the most-successful and longest-running movie franchises in the world. And things will remain that way in the years to come.

Duel of the Players

Bond on the Hunt for Ian Fleming's Cousin

56

After *You Only Live Twice*, Ian Fleming continues the story of 007. In the novel *The Man with the Golden Gun*, Bond is suffering from amnesia after being injured after falling from Blofeld's fortress—and he has been brainwashed by the Soviets. His mission: to kill M. He fails in this assignment—for the only time in his career—and MI6 is able to overpower him and "wash him clean" again. He is actually not fit for duty but is assigned to a suicide mission by M, in order to eliminate the notorious killer Scaramanga. In the movie, Bond comes to the same mission by a very different route. This time, Scaramanga's lover has sent him a hidden message.

Francisco Scaramanga is played by the impressive Christopher Lee, who—what a twist of fate!—had himself worked as a liaison officer for the British secret service, the Special Operations Executive (SOE), during World War II. So in a broader sense, Lee was a colleague of the fictional 007, but there was another connection to James Bond as well. Because Lee's mother had married a brother

In May 1953, Ian Fleming had corrected the proofs for *Live and Let Die* while he was on board the RMS *Queen Elizabeth*. In 1972, the ship was destroyed by a fire when it was in the port of Hong Kong; it was then used as an outpost for MI6 in the movie.
Image: Barry Loigman / CC BY-SA 2.5

A showdown that turns into a game of deception. Scaramanga has challenged James Bond to a duel and plays by his own rules. *Image: Picture Alliance*

of Ian Fleming's mother, the two were cousins. Fleming had previously proposed Lee to play Dr. No in the first James Bond movie, but the production company had already filled the role.

A Duel in a Vacation Paradise

Scaramanga always keeps himself one step ahead of Bond throughout the movie. Then the British secret agent seeks the killer on his idyllic island—right in the lion's den. The duel that Scaramanga is offering is not on equal footing, because the man with the golden gun knows all the tricks and traps of his hideout. His gadgets make him really able to compete with Q during the entire movie. But his vanity ends up cooking his goose. He had a wax figure made of Bond that he likes to use for target practice. So he ends up losing against two Bonds, because the real 007 has taken the position of the figure and is able to take the villain out.

The Weapon of Francisco S.

Ingenious, Gold, and Temporary

57

Since he had to do a lot of traveling as an international hit man, Francisco Scaramanga needed a suitable weapon. A brilliant Portuguese gunsmith living in the former colony of Macau in China made him an impressive device for his work. The weapon was ideal for smuggling because it was made up of various items in everyday use: a cigarette lighter, a cigarette case, a fountain pen, and a cuff link for the trigger. In the movie *In the Line of Fire*, made nineteen years later, the villain played by John Malkovich owned a similar weapon, although his was made of plastic (plus, in 2003, some ten years later, Malkovich played the main villain Pascal Sauvage in the first of the Johnny English movies). But now back to Scaramanga's gun in the movie: this ingenious single-shot weapon was a pistol and was made by Lazar, the Macau gunsmith.

Assassin Francisco Scaramanga operates from the shadows with his unique single-shot golden gun.

Scaramanga's golden gun (replica), and golden gun bullet, *The Man with the Golden Gun*, 1974

Courtesy the Museum of World War II, Boston

Scaramanga's pistol, made from various individual parts that would not arouse suspicion by themselves, was able to fire only a single shot, and then he had to reload it. *Image: Gareth Milner*

Christopher Lee convincingly played the movie villain Francisco Scaramanga. His watch and his chunky ring also prove his love for gold. *Image: Picture Alliance*

Another One Who Loves Gold

Francisco Scaramanga has a great passion that makes him a spiritual brother to Goldfinger: he loves the gleaming precious metal of gold. He has a gold watch and a gold ring, and he fires gold cartridges. It is only logical that his handgun would also be made of this material.

Nick Nack

A Small Enemy Can Also Be Dangerous

58

The Frenchman and midget named Nick Nack was more of a majordomo than a servant to the man with the golden gun. The character, whose name is essentially a diminutive for "knickknack," was an invention of the scriptwriters, since he does not appear in the novel. A classy invention, because this crafty and diminutive man is loyal but keeps challenging his boss again and again, knowing full well that he will meet the challenges. Right at the beginning of the movie, we see Nick Nack sitting at a control desk with monitors, directing Scaramanga's duel with the crook Rodney. Nick Nack keeps putting his boss up against obstacles, which the sharpshooter overcomes with aplomb. Nick Nack also provides support for Scaramanga during his missions; for example, Nick Nack steals the Solex device that Scaramanga needs for his solar-powered laser cannon. Nick Nack's ultimate end is not clear, because Bond is able to capture him and tie him to the top of the mast.

Hervé Villechaize, the actor who played the diminutive villain, was apparently no slouch, because he is said to have hit on both Maud Adams and Britt Ekland

(unsuccessfully). The Parisian actor starred in the television series *Fantasy Island* from 1977 to 1983. Unfortunately, he suffered from serious health problems that even made it impossible for him to get a healthy amount of sleep. He drowned the pain resulting from his severe stomach ulcer in alcohol. On September 5, 1993, he shot himself while intoxicated in his adopted home state of California.

The diminutive French actor Hervé Villechaize played Scaramanga's most important accomplice.
Image: Collection of Michael Dörflinger

Cars That Can Even Fly

Spectacular Vehicle Stunts

Much of the movie version of *The Man with a Golden Gun* is set in Thailand, including a memorable car chase. Bond steals an AMC Hornet, which just happens to have the cranky Louisiana sheriff J. W. Pepper sitting in it, whom we already know from *Live and Let Die*. Scaramanga and Nick Nack retreat into a barn, and it seems as if they are caught in a trap—but then the barn doors open, and their AMC Matador, remodeled into an airplane, rises into the air. Scaramanga's flying car used in the movie was just a model. Because flying automobiles were already known to audiences from such movies as *Fantomas Unleashed*, produced in France in 1965, *The Man with the Golden Gun* features an even more spectacular stunt, performed by Bond's double during the car chase along the Klong Rangsit canal near Bangkok. The Bond stuntman drives the AMC Hornet over a bridge that has been broken in two, executing a corkscrew turn that rotates the car 360 degrees around its own longitudinal axis. It cost $300,000 to work out how to do the stunt by using elaborate calculations on a computer. It worked the first time the stuntman did it. They didn't do a second take because the driver refused.

The AMC Hornet X that James Bond stole is whiling away its golden years in a museum. No one will ever forget the corkscrew turn stunt it performed when the Bond stuntman drove it over a half-destroyed wooden bridge. *Image: Fri / CC BY-SA 4.0*

Where Scaramanga Lived

They Still Call It James Bond Island Today

60

In the book, Scaramanga was to be found on Ian Fleming's favorite island of Jamaica, and most of the plot is set there. In the movie, however, the villain makes his home on the Thai island of Khao Phing Kan in Phang Nga Bay, near the well-known vacation destination of Phuket.

In the movie, the island where Scaramanga has his luxuriously furnished dwelling looks like a holiday paradise, but conditions were much more spartan while they were making the movie. There were no toilets and no running water. At the same time, it was extremely hot. Christopher Lee, who appeared to be well tanned in this movie, in reality was not. His career of playing Dracula meant lots of lying around in coffins and sleeping while the sun was shining, apparently leaving his complexion very pale. So he used makeup to appear more tan. Because the makeup kept dripping off in the heat, he had to constantly reapply it. Of course, no one stayed on the island overnight. Some of the crew flew to work by helicopter, while others arrived by boat.

Khao Phing Kan Today

Crowds of tourists continue to visit the island, even years after the movie premiered. They take photos of the rock needle, see that there would never have been the space to build a Scaramanga palace there, and leave their trash lying around. James Bond is both a blessing and a curse here. Incidentally, the

James Bond flew this Republic RC-3 Seabee seaplane, identifier number N87545, to the luxurious lair of the killer Scaramanga to rescue his colleague Mary Goodnight. The plane was destroyed as the plot unfolded. *Image: Bill Larkins / CC BY-SA 2.0*

In the movie, the rock rising in front of Scaramanga's island housed a solar power plant. Today the island is one of the most popular tourist destinations in Thailand. *Image: Collection of Michael Dörflinger*

"James Bond Island" makes an appearance in another 007 movie. When Pierce Brosnan as James Bond is making his way to Elliot Carver's stealth ship, if you look closely you can recognize the island in the background.

In 1974, everyone was talking about solar energy, which plays a special role for the island in the movie. Due to the "Oil Shock" crisis and its consequences, which made citizens aware of what could happen if they did not have a secure energy source, efforts to develop this technology had increased significantly.

James Bond as a Tourist Magnet

The "Bond Island" is not the only location used in the movie franchise that is now being used commercially. In the Bahamas, for example, there was the beach bar and grill featured in *Never Say Never Again*, which was built by the proprietors of the hotel where the film crew was living. On the island, visitors have the opportunity to dive for the bomber sunk at that time or a shipwreck. In Jamaica, the Jamaica Safari Village advertises itself using the famous scene in which Bond jumps across three crocodiles as "stepping-stones" to save himself from these ravenous beasts in *Live and Let Die*. On page 152, you can read how 007's bungee jump in *GoldenEye* is turned into a money earner.

For Your Eyes Only

From the Short Story to the Movie

61

Now, as you all know well, "for your eyes only" means something along the lines of "top secret." The original English title refers to Ian Fleming's short story of the same name, but the movie used hardly any of this material. All the same, it does include a Bond girl with the last name of Havelock, who wants to avenge the murder of her parents. For the first time, this adventure was based on a short story instead of a novel. But by now, the filmmakers had almost completely emancipated themselves from Fleming's prototypes. Elements that had proven their worth, such as a fantastic car chase or a hunt on skis, were written into the screenplay. The real villain is a supposedly well-meaning person. A little treat for Bond fans showed up only later on: Cassandra Harris, who finds herself in Moore's arms as Countess Lisl, was at the time married to Pierce Brosnan—who later played Bond himself.

This rust-red Lotus was the successor to the white Lotus Esprit S1 as James Bond's company car. Here Roger Moore poses beside it wearing a 007 jacket. *Image: Picture Alliance / ©United Artists / Courtesy Everett Collection*

Sheena Makes an Appearance
From 007 to *Miami Vice*?

It was a generational change. After Shirley Bassey sang the theme for *Moonraker*, a new face would take over for the next movie. And that is to be taken literally, because the singer Sheena Easton, who interpreted the theme for *For Your Eyes Only*, appeared over and over again in the opening credits. That had never happened before or since. The then-twenty-two-year-old Scottish singer had made her breakthrough only a year earlier with her single "Modern Girl." Her appearance in the British reality television series *The Big Time*, where the camera followed her first steps in show business, made this acting and music student a star. One of her promoters was Dusty Springfield (see page 36), whose song "The Look of Love" was featured in the 1967 version of *Casino Royale*. Easton's second single, "9 to 5 (Morning Train)," brought her up to number 1 on the US charts, but in Great Britain she only got to third place.

It had quickly became clear that Sheena Easton should sing the new Bond song. The song came out the following year and reached number 1 in Switzerland, the Netherlands, and Norway. The title was nominated for an Oscar in the Best Song category in 1982 but lost out to "Arthur's Theme" by Christopher Cross.

In 1987, Sheena Easton surprised everyone with her appearance in the TV series *Miami Vice*. The series' success was based on many elements also found in the 007 franchise: fast cars and boats, luxury, the beach, and beautiful women,

The back of the record sleeve for Sheena Easton's successful single, which climbed up to first place in Switzerland.
Image: Collection of Michael Dörflinger

with suspense and villains added to the mix. In the series, she married the star Sonny Crockett, but soon has to die. During 2015–16, she performed in symphonic concerts with the title "The Spy Who Loved Me," which featured songs from secret-agent movies.

The Real Citroën "Duck" Is Yellow

... and Is Shot Full of Holes

63

When one thing comes to an end, there is always also an opportunity for something new. This also applies to the legendary white Lotus Esprit that James Bond had been driving as his company car since *The Spy Who Loved Me*. The car falls into the hands of Bond's antagonists, and it reacts with the ultimate defensive tactic: it explodes. Any well-trained secret agent's car would rather get blown sky high than let the villains see its interior. This means that 007 is left without a set of wheels. Now he can show just what he's made of.

A Duck Dance à la 007

Bond flees with Melina Havelock in her yellow "Duck," a Citroën 2CV car from the property of the criminal Hector Gonzales, who is located near Madrid. But the scenes were shot on the island of Corfu. As they are pursued by two black Renaults, Bond quickly realizes that Melina's best qualities do not lie in fast driving but rather in archery. So he takes over the wheel and performs the most incredible stunts in a vehicle he knows absolutely nothing about. Here Bond is played by the actual champion driver Rémy Julienne. Bond's two pursuers are also driving French cars: two Peugeot 504s, which operate in a higher class in terms of performance. So it all depends on the driver. The Duck finds its final

To mark the occasion of the James Bond movie, Citroën released the special "James Bond" model 2 CV 1981—featuring glued-on bullet holes and the 007 logo on its doors.
Image: Newspress

With a bit of luck, you will be able to spot a Citroën Duck featuring the 007 look at a classic car meet. It certainly is cheaper than buying a DB5. *Image: Beaulieu Enterprises / Newspress*

parking place in the Corfiot mountain village of Pagi, where it overturns and lands right in the middle of a fruit vendor's stand. Years later, this stunt was still a popular topic of conversation at the fruit stand in the village.

Of course, a real Citroën Duck would never have been able to create such scenes. The technicians of the film crew came up with a lot of ideas to turn this bird with a broken wing into a yellow roadrunner. The factory engine was replaced with a four-cylinder boxer engine taken from the Citroën GS model. This model was a family car, which had some technical refinements of the legendary DS. The engine performance on Melina's Duck was thus more than double that of the production model. Other equipment was added on, of course, especially powerful cross shock absorbers and a roll bar.

The Bond Car for the Normal Person

In 1981, Citroën finally fulfilled the secret wishes of many Bond car fans.

Its special edition of the 2 CV, with a yellow paint job bearing the 007 logo and glued-on bullet holes, finally made one of the revered agent's cars affordable. Exactly how many of these cars were made is not known. Reports are that it was around a thousand. However, the buyers had to do without the more powerful engine on the movie vehicle and all the extras.

The Citroën 2 CV6 – "007"	
Production period:	1981
Power output:	21 kW
Length:	165 inches (4,191 mm)
Height:	43.75 inches (1,111 mm)
Width:	73.25 inches (1,861 mm)
Top speed:	71 mph (115 km/h)

A View to a Kill

This Is Where Opinions Diverge

It's a glamorous ensemble of stars. Christopher Walken is Max Zorin, an unscrupulous entrepreneur. Tanya Roberts, who plays Stacey Sutton, was one of the "angels" on the *Charlie's Angels* TV series during 1980–81 and had already played a superhero herself as the scantily clad female version of Tarzan in *Sheena: Queen of the Jungle* in 1984. And then there was Grace Jones. The singer was not only allowed to show what she could do in this movie, but she also brought her bodyguard and lover Dolph Lundgren along with her, who was able to slip into the role of the KGB henchman Venz. A year later, he beat up Sylvester Stallone in *Rocky IV* and became an action star.

The Older Man and Everyone Else

And then there was also Roger Moore. If everyone had already been making fun of the "aged" Sean Connery, this was all the more true for Moore, who was fifty-seven years old at the time. For many, he was no longer tenable as James Bond (but he would be retiring young when you consider that Q still had to earn his bread at age eighty-five). As a result, for some the movie just can't do anything right, while others love it—not least because of stunts such as May Day's parachute jump from the Eiffel Tower, the fire truck chase through San Francisco, and the great shots in Zorin's mine. The opening sequence, as so often happens, involves a mission in the Soviet Union, and Willy Bogner and his ski team are once again able to show off their skills. Bond has to flee on skis and then on a snowmobile runner, which he "repurposes" into a snowboard. There is no lack of humor. Especially when Bond, disguised as the horse lover James St. John Smythe, sneaks into Zorin's stud farm at the latter's chateau, assisted by his colleague Sir Godfrey Tibbett (played by actor Patrick Macnee), who pretends to be the chauffeur.

When it came to the **gadgets**, it was too much of a good thing for many viewers. An electric razor to detect electronic bugs, and glasses that let you see through mirrored glass: OK. Then a ring with a camera and a credit card that silences alarm systems: certainly. But a submarine disguised as an iceberg and a remote-controlled robot dog that contains a camera that Q can use to monitor Bond? Opinions are split here.

Christopher Walken, Grace Jones, and Tanya Roberts flanking Bond actor Roger Moore at a press conference. Image: *Picture Alliance / United Archives / IFTN*

Duran Duran Sings about 007

The First Bond Number 1 in the US Charts

After a getaway to Hollywood and Bill Conti's movie score for *For Your Eyes Only*, which sounded more like Rocky than James Bond, when it came to *Octopussy* and *A View to a Kill*, filmmakers brought back the old warhorse and Oscar winner John Barry, who had already arranged the musical theme for the very first Bond movie. Overall, he was responsible for the sound for twelve movies in the franchise. For the title song of *A View to a Kill*, Roger Moore's last outing as 007, Barry wrote a song together with the pop group Duran Duran that achieved something that had never been done before: a James Bond theme song made it to number 1 on the US charts.

A year after their hit "Wild Boys," the synthpop band Duran Duran was able to sing the theme song for the new James Bond movie.
Image: Collection of Michael Dörflinger

Duran Duran was founded in the late 1970s and was dedicated to the New Wave emerging at the time. With titles such as "Girls on Film" and "The Wild Boys," the group was especially popular with teenyboppers. The idea was to win this increasingly affluent target group over for James Bond. When making the next movie in the franchise, *The Living Daylights*, filmmakers tried to repeat the same formula for success for the title song and brought A-ha on board. The Norwegian band had stormed the hit parades in 1985 with its single "Take on Me." Pål Waaktaar, the guitarist of this pop group built around the charismatic vocalist Morten Harket, wrote the Bond song together with John Barry.

James Bond was certainly a theme for some other musical groups as well. In 1990, the Berlin-based ska band Blechreiz released an album—titled *Who Napped J.B.?* —which includes the song "James Bond." The English band the Selecter had released a song of the same name back in 1980. Both take up on Monty Norman's Bond anthem. Even Bruce Willis released a single in 1987: "Secret Agent Man (James Bond Is Back)."

The fatal finale of Roger Moore's last Bond movie was played out on this bridge. Max Zorin in his airship did not stand a chance against 007. *Image: Andreas Amend*

Endgame on the Bridge

The Fight for Life and Death 746 Feet in the Air

Everyone was talking about Silicon Valley in 1985. This center of the global computer industry, located in a suburb of San Francisco, was the target chosen by villain Max Zorin. Zorin, who was born in Dresden, Germany, is the progeny of breeding experiments by the former Nazi Carl Mortner (in the German version of the movie, Mortner has morphed into a Polish KGB agent). These artificially bred people have enormously high IQs but often become psychopaths. It's a dangerous mixture that only a very experienced secret agent would be able to stand up to . . .

66

Bond defeats the ax-wielding Zorin in a battle on one of the two suspension cables of the Golden Gate Bridge, and Zorin plunges into San Francisco Bay. The initial intention was to have him fall onto one of the traffic lanes, but the city refused this idea because it was feared it might lead to a wave of suicides. Zorin's airship—which has a British registration, by the way—explodes. It wasn't only James Bond who won out in this adventure; the city of San Francisco also profited by collecting $5 million for giving the moviemakers permission to film there.

Olga Kurylenko, the Avenging Angel

Daniel Craig Needs a Quantum of Solace

67

In 2008, a new Fleming title was used as the name for a movie for the first time since 1987's *The Living Daylights*: *Quantum of Solace*. *Casino Royale* comes in between, but that title had already been used before. *Quantum of Solace* sounds a bit strange. Even Daniel Craig had to get used to it at first. But he must have quickly realized what it meant when he first met Olga Kurylenko, who plays the female lead role and is certainly the highlight of an otherwise rather boring movie.

She plays Camille, a Bolivian secret agent who has a dark secret because General Medrano, the accomplice of the main villain Dominic Greene, had murdered her family. A reference to Camille as the avenging angel can also be found in the passage in the movie that plays out on the floating opera stage on Lake Constance at Bregenz, Austria. Like Tosca, the central character of the opera being performed there, she too will kill a villain. Interestingly, in 2018, Olga Kurylenko starred in the Bond parody *Johnny English Strikes Again*.

When it comes to beautiful women, James Bond has no reservations. He will even get into a small Ford Ka and let the lady take the wheel. *Image: Karen Ballard / Newspress*

A classy brand ambassador for Ford. This Frenchwoman with Ukrainian roots became known for her action movies based on computer games. *Quantum of Solace* still remains the high point of her acting career. *Image: Newspress*

Ford Makes a 007 Mobile

Riding Shotgun in the New Ford Ka

68

James Bond movies are always a super platform for promoting new products. Besides Aston Martin and BMW, the car company that has promoted itself more than any other in the Bond universe is the American manufacturer Ford (see page 23). *Quantum of Solace* introduces a cute minicar, which became known as the "car with a soul." In ancient Egypt, the Ka was the part of a soul that gives the life force. This was something that James Bond needed urgently (see page 134).

A Little City Runabout

The first generation of the Ford Ka appeared in 1996. This subcompact car with its striking rounded design was manufactured in Ford's Spanish plant in the town of Almussafes. The Ka was also introduced in South America in 1997, where it was manufactured in the Brazilian city of São Bernardo do Campo. In technical terms, the Ka was a relative of the Ford Fiesta and shares

Camille was lucky—she got to drive the new Ford Ka even before its market launch. The weathered hotel name shows that the action is taking place in Haiti. *Image: Newspress*

The Ford Ka on the set. For the American car manufacturer, having the new model make its premiere in a James Bond movie created an extremely successful advertising presence. *Image: Newspress*

the Fiesta's mechanical underpinnings. The four-cylinder engine was available in versions generating 44, 51, and 70 kW. In 2009, the first generation of the model was replaced by the Ka II, which had already been seen a year earlier in Daniel Craig's second Bond escapade.

The Prototype as a Movie Star

Ford developed the car together with Fiat on the basis of the latter's Panda model. Unlike its predecessor, this Ka had very few flaws. The car also fits this movie in another way, because we could say that the small size of the car body symbolizes the length of the movie. *Quantum of Solace* is the shortest movie in the Bond franchise, running just 106 minutes. The movie has nothing to do with the Ian Fleming short story of the same name. Even so, a car also makes an appearance in Fleming's story: a Morris that the betrayed husband gives to his wife when they separate. However, he has made hardly any of the installment payments for it.

Ford Ka (RU8)	
Production period:	2008–2016
Power output:	51 kW
Length:	142.5 inches (3,620 mm)
Height:	59.25 inches (1,505 mm)
Width:	65.3 inches (1,658 mm)
Top speed:	99 mph (159 km/h)

In the Mountains and by the Sea

James Bond Seeks Life

69

Marc Forster, the director of *Quantum of Solace*, once said, "In a way the most interesting place for a James Bond movie to go is inward, deeper into Bond himself." This journey now has greater appeal than the exotic locations, Forster said. Of course, this was not to say that the plots taking Bond to a range of countries would now be dispensed with. Bond still gets around a lot in this flick. Right away in the opening sequence, he gets involved in a wild chase race in Italy, involving two Alfas driving from Lake Garda to Tuscany, plus he cruises around the harbor of Port-au-Prince in a boat, experiences the open-air opera stage at Bregenz on Lake Constance, and pursues his antagonist all the way to a South American desert.

James Bond is a wreck after losing his beloved Vesper Lynd in *Casino Royale*—almost as much of a wreck as the beached boat shown in the photo below. He has captured the murderous Mr. White, who killed Le Chiffre in that movie, and in the car chase described above brings White from Lake Garda to Siena for interrogation.

The boat that Bond—or, rather, a stuntman—sailed in *Quantum of Solace* was on display at Buckler's Hard village in the county of Hampshire, England. *Image: Newspress*

Bond was able to shake off his pursuers in the marble quarries of Carrara, Italy.
Image: Michael Dörflinger

Trust is a recurring theme of this movie. In a job where feints, secrets, and deception are the order of the day, trust is something hard to do. Bond has trusted. He trusted Vesper Lynd—and she betrayed him. And he trusts M. But she mistrusts 007 and has him followed and blocks his accounts. She doesn't believe him because she suspects he has plans for revenge. This is a dark and brooding Bond, someone who cowers in the dark and waits. There are no humorous scenes to be found.

A Sinister Hero

In this film, the scriptwriters give Bond only a single bedroom scene—with a lady named Strawberry Fields, of all things. Her parents must have been Beatles fans, because this of course is the name of a song by Liverpool's "Fab Four." Before this, it was only the television Bond of 1954 who got so little time for relaxation. And what happens with Camille? That is up to the viewer. But it looks as if she could well ultimately be Bond's quantum of solace. And he could also be hers.

Mission in Germany

James Bond Visits East and West

70

The death of a clown in the British embassy in Berlin turns out to be the murder of one of James Bond's colleagues: 009. He had smuggled a Czarist-era jeweled Fabergé egg from St. Petersburg into the West but was murdered by two knife throwers. Along with an art expert from MI6, 007 is assigned to observe the auction of the egg at Sotheby's auction house. This is a scene (including the Fabergé egg) taken from Ian Fleming's "The Property of a Lady," a short story from the same volume in which "Octopussy" was also published.

The scene became part of the *Octopussy* film. Longer passages of the movie subsequently take place in India, but then the action returns to Germany. 007 meets M on Kurfürstendamm avenue in Berlin and then travels to East Germany. The Octopussy circus troupe is appearing in the city of Chemnitz, which at that time was still called Karl-Marx-Stadt.

A Soviet Warmonger Takes On His Own Government

General Orlov's plan is to detonate an atomic bomb in West Germany in order to create panic in the peace movement in the NATO area of operations and thus reinforce it. After western Europe disarms in reaction to the bomb, his troops could then march in. The bomb is supposed to be planted on Octopussy's circus train. They were told the lie that they would be smuggling jewelry. The train's destination, the US base at "Feldstadt," must lie in the German region of Franconia, which is in Bavaria; in any case, the car license plates from the regional

The *Octopussy* Boat

One of Ian Fleming's neighbors in Jamaica was named Blanche Blackwell. She was the mother of Chris Blackwell, who later founded Island Records, a record label that initially signed reggae musicians and later stars such as U2, Robert Palmer, and Grace Jones. Her relationship with Fleming was not only neighborly but, as Bond would say, "deeper." It is said that she was the role model for Pussy Galore and Honey Ryder. Blanche Blackwell, who died in 2017 at the age of 104, had given Ian Fleming a boat that was named the *Octopussy*. Other sources say he gave the boat to her. In any case, both of them sailed in it together.

Roger Moore in front of Checkpoint Charlie at the border between West and East Berlin. The East-West conflict plays a major role in *Octopussy*. *Image: Picture Alliance / © United Artists / courtesy Everett Collection*

cities of Bayreuth and Nuremberg indicate this. Against all odds, James Bond—also disguised as a clown, which takes up the plot of the opening sequence again—is able to defuse the bomb. But that's not the end of it all, because the action goes back to India, where the Octopussy ladies attack the villain Kamal Khan. Bond, who is with Q in a patriotic tethered balloon sporting a Union Jack design, intervenes to save the day. Then comes the grandiose finale in and around Khan's private plane.

Checkpoint Charlie in Berlin, where Roger Moore is shown in the picture above, plays an important role in the story "The Living Daylights." The location was moved to Bratislava in Slovakia in the movie version of *The Living Daylights*, based on this story. *Octopussy* gets a lot of mileage out of national cliches: in India there are snake charmers, sword swallowers, and fakir's beds of nails—all of which are cleverly integrated into a chase in Tuk Tuks (auto rickshaws). No Bond comes without **gadgets**, and there are quite a few in *Octopussy*. First and foremost is the artificial crocodile Bond uses as cover so he can swim to Octopussy's palace undetected. In Q's lab, they are working on a rope trick and a deadly door with spikes, as well as a fountain pen that can dissolve metals and be used for communications. But the villains also have their tools. Notable is the yo-yo saw used by the assassin in Octopussy's bedroom.

Micro Jet at the Gas Station

The Ultimate Opening-Sequence Gag

The opening sequences have developed into classic elements of James Bond movies, telling the story of a completely different 007 mission. In *Octopussy*, the opening takes Roger Moore to Cuba. He sneaks into a Cuban air force base disguised as an officer. When it seems that the operation has failed, Bond is able to escape and turns the mission into a grandiose success when flying his micro jet. As he does so, he runs into the very person he had pretended to be so that he could penetrate the base: Colonel Toro Der. The character is played by an old friend of Roger Moore's: the man who played his double in *The Saint*. The resemblance between the two is really amazing.

The micro jet was not an invention of the 007 technicians. It really existed! This plane is a Bede BD-5J, a single-seater available in kit form, powered by a Microturbo TRS-18 jet engine. Jim Bede, who developed the aircraft, took off on its maiden flight in 1971. This first model still had a motor with a pusher propeller. This version of a jet plane, nicknamed the "Acrostar Jet," was the smallest jet aircraft in the world at the time. It reached a speed of 300 mph (480 km/h).

The Bede BD-5J micro jet, the Acrostar Jet, filling up at the gas station. The idea for the flip-up wings as an "extra option" came from Q's department. *Image: Picture Alliance*

Another airplane also plays an important role at the end of the movie. This time, Bond is chasing after the fleeing Kamal Khan and his helper Gobinda, who have just taken off and have kidnapped Octopussy. Bond manages to hold on tight to the plane as it takes off, throw Gobinda down from it, and rescue Octopussy. Khan's aircraft was a Beechcraft 18 C-45H Expeditor, built in 1951, and already an older model at that time. In reality, of course, it didn't explode. The twin-engine aircraft, bearing the registration G-BKRG and with US Air Force paintwork, is now parked at Lelystad Aviodrome in the Netherlands, the country's national aviation museum.

On the Nene Valley Railway

A Little East Germany in Eastern England

72

It wasn't possible to film the railroad scenes in *Octopussy* in the German Democratic Republic (GDR)—East Germany—although there were still many steam locomotives in regular service there at that time. Instead, the moviemakers used the Nene Valley Railway in east-central England in place of East Germany. The Wansford and Ferry Meadows stations played particularly important roles during the filming. This is where the moviemakers set up their own "Inner German Border." It was also the place where James Bond drove along the tracks on the tire rims of a Mercedes to catch up with the train. The number of the German locomotive, 62 015, is a real one, but the locomotive is the Swedish DSB S (II) 740, which had been sold to the Nene Valley Railway in 1979.

A few years later, the scenes involving Alec Trevelyan's armored train were filmed here when making *GoldenEye*. The Russian diesel locomotive is played by a British Rail Class 20 counterpart. The Nene Valley Railway, which is approximately 7.5 miles (12 kilometers) long, was opened in 1977 as a museum railway. It includes five train stations.

The railroad scenes taking place at the station were filmed in Wansford Station on the Nene Valley Railway. It was here that they also built an "Inner German Border." *Image: Duncan Harris / CC BY-SA 2.0*

Bond and Mercedes? Somehow, that never became a theme. As a rule, the black Mercedes limousines were reserved for the villains. In *Octopussy,* however, 007 uses General Orlov's car to board the train in a rather unconventional way. *Image: Picture Alliance*

Rumors about the New Bond

From the Shakespearean Stage to the Wide World

73

The whole world was excitedly waiting to see who would take on the role of the famous English secret agent 007 after Roger Moore. The choice fell on Timothy Dalton, who had been known for playing classical roles up until then. He was supposed to present "another kind" of Bond, one who bore a closer resemblance to the character in the books.

The Living Daylights begins with an operational drill on the Rock of Gibraltar. MI6 drops off three agents there to test the security capacity of a new radar system, but who is the new James Bond? The first one you see looks a bit like Roger Moore. But he doesn't live very long. Another one looks a bit like George Lazenby. He doesn't make it either. Ultimately, it is Timothy Dalton. After a long fight, he is able

The action-packed opening sequences of the first Bond flick featuring Timothy Dalton are set on the Rock of Gibraltar. *Image: Michael Dörflinger*

to take out the assassin. The plot is not entirely made up out of thin air, because it refers to Ian Fleming's own deployment in World War II. During the war, Operation "Goldeneye" attempted to protect the Strait of Gibraltar from radar surveillance by the Germans. In 1940, Fleming himself was stationed in the Overseas Territory, a British exclave, for this operation.

The Living Daylights is based on the short story of the same name, which revolves around a defector from the Soviet Union. Cello player Kara Milvoy is supposed to shoot the defector at the inner border dividing East and West Germany. Bond discovers her in time but does not kill her; he just puts her out of action. The movie plot is built on this story. But Kara is not a murderer here;

rather, she was only helping her boyfriend, Koskov, to make it look like an assassination attempt in order to lull the Western agents into a false sense of security. Actually, he is a traitor.

The high point of the movie is certainly the car chase featuring the Aston Martin V-8. Bond is able to make use of all sorts of new **gadgets** in the car. It ends with a spectacular ride using Kara's cello case as a sled. For this mission, 007 got not only the famous Aston Martin from Q's laboratory, but also a very special key

At the premiere of *The Living Daylights*, Timothy Dalton and movie villain Jeroen Krabbé have no reason to be at odds. *Image: Bart Molendijk / Anefo*

finder. Depending on the melody Bond would whistle, it could explode, stun people with gas, or—find a key. Equipped with these gadgets, he prevails. Arms dealer Whitaker is killed, and the traitor Koskov is arrested. At the end, Kara is able to play in a widely acclaimed concert in Vienna: her career has begun.

James Bond's Aston Martin (see page 144) and the famous cello case he and Kara used to flee down the mountain and across the border into Austria. *Image: Karen Roe / CC BY-SA 3.0*

The Aston Martin V-8 Vantage

Yet Another Carful of Gadgets

74

After taking a long break of many years during the movies starring Roger Moore, James Bond was finally driving an Aston Martin again in *The Living Daylights*. The V-8 Vantage came out a year before the movie was made—so Q had enough time to install all of his **gadgets**. These included a laser that can burn through metal—which he demonstrates by cutting the car body out of a Czechoslovak police vehicle.

The car also boasts two missiles, which Bond deploys using a head-up display. The missiles are fired from the front fog lights. The tires have retractable spikes, and besides all this, the V-8

The Aston Martin V8 Vantage	
Production period:	1986–1989
Power output:	308 kW
Length:	180.5 inches (4,585 mm)
Height:	52.4 inches (1,330 mm)
Width:	72 inches (1,830 mm)
Top speed:	168 mph (270 km/h)

For the winter scenes, Bond drove a hardtop V-8 Vantage. At the beginning, he was still driving a convertible car. *Image: Aston Martin*

Vantage also boasts a rocket engine, extendable skids on the sides, and a self-destruct function with timer. The car demonstrates all it can do on the wintry border between Czechoslovakia and Austria. The drive across the frozen lake became the model for the car chase in *Die Another Day*. The vehicle's name is a play on words: "Vee Eight Vantage" said out loud makes you think of "advantage." The open convertible version of the Aston Martin V-8 Vantage Volante could reach a top speed of 168 mph (270 km/h). At the time, this made it the fastest mass-produced convertible in the world.

But Bond's car is destroyed, certainly to Q's great regret. Q will have to console himself with other gadgets from his workshop, such as his boom-box rocket launcher or the sofa that eats people. James Bond then maneuvers his way through the rest of the movie in German cars: two Audi 200s. The Audi 200 Quattro belonging to his colleague Saunders, which Bond drives when in Bratislava, can be admired today in the company's own Audi Museum in Ingolstadt, Bavaria.

Revenge Instead of a 00 Mission

Probably the Worst Bond Movie Ever

There actually was no novel that served as the basis for the movie *License to Kill*, but a lot of the motifs were distilled from the novels *Live and Let Die* and *The Man with the Golden Gun*. The plot does not really involve a mission either, since Dalton's James Bond sets out to hunt down a gang that mutilated his friend Felix Leiter and murdered Leiter's new wife. In this film, Bond is thus very much in the tradition of the vigilante justice movies that were particularly well liked in the 1980s and made very popular by Charles Bronson.

Totally New Character Traits

To exact this revenge, Bond misses an assignment. M confronts him at the Ernest Hemingway house in Key West and even shies away from having Bond liquidated only because of the passersby. Otherwise, he would

Ernest Hemingway's former home in Key West was the scene of James Bond's ugly farewell to M and MI6. *Image: Collection of Michael Dörflinger*

A dangerous Bond stunt involving a fuel tanker filled with drugs. The explosive finale of 007's off-duty vendetta campaign is energetically supported by CIA agent Pam Bouvier in a Piper PA-18 Super Cub. *Image: Picture Alliance / Richter Collection*

mercilessly have had Bond shot. However, it remains unclear why Bond does not want to hand over his pistol, and thus he escalates his expulsion. In fact, he could have found a weapon anywhere. This is the beginning of his new relationship with M, which will continue to spin through the series with M's woman successor. Not only is the name of the primary villain, Franz Sanchez, similar to that of Francisco Scaramanga in the novel *The Man with the Golden Gun*, Sanchez also plays a very similar role in the movie.

How Bond Got a License to Kill

An agent gets the "double O" status, as the James Bond of the novel explains in *Casino Royale*, when they are ready to kill and have killed two persons. Bond got his license to kill because he had killed a Japanese man working as a code specialist in New York and a Norwegian double agent in Stockholm. *Casino Royale*, starring Daniel Craig, shows these two "double O" killings in the opening sequence. Bond kills an evildoer in a bathroom, and the traitorous section head in Prague.

Pierce Brosnan Takes Over

An Irishman Plays Britain's Top Agent

76

Remington Steele was a straw man. The woman private detective Laura Holt was barely able to get any assignments and realized that this could be due to the fact that as a woman, people would not trust her with them. So she comes up with Remington Steele, and Pierce Brosnan plays the impostor who is the face of the detective agency. Suddenly the clients are coming in droves. Steele becomes more and more of a detective himself. This series ran on television for many years and prevented Brosnan from being engaged to play James Bond. As early as 1983, a majority had voted in a poll in favor of Pierce Brosnan becoming Roger Moore's successor. Finally, the time had come with *GoldenEye*. But people had to wait a long time for the Brosnan Bond because the second Dalton movie had led to a lot of disagreements, and the producers had to consider what they could do better. Therefore, it took six years until the filming began. The moviemakers went to great lengths to produce *GoldenEye* because nothing more or less than the future of the entire Bond franchise was at stake.

A lot had changed: James Bond no longer smokes and now has a woman for a boss, who is in no way inferior to her predecessor in terms of arrogance. There wasn't any novel by Ian Fleming that could be used for the filming here, but filmmakers helped themselves from the stock of motifs and characters. Alec "Janus" Trevelyan is a typical Bond villain with a physical defect. For him, it is his half-burned face. In the opening sequence, he is still acting as if he is

Pierce Brosnan is an actor who really can wear suits well. His natural elegance was very well received by audiences, especially women.
Image: BMW/Newspress

The film team returned to the Nene Valley Railway to shoot *GoldenEye;* the railway had already been used for shooting *Octopussy. Image: Picture Alliance / Richter Collection*

Bond's friend and colleague; apparently he was shot while on a mission. But years later he reemerges as Janus and is planning a great criminal act. To do this, he needs the GoldenEye, a satellite system that can do battle with targets on the earth. The name is taken from Fleming's deployment during World War II and his villa in Jamaica. Trevelyan's headquarters, on the armored train, was taken from *Diamonds Are Forever*, but in that story the villain has a luxury train.

In the James Bond movie *GoldenEye*, you can admire the Z3 Roadster 2.8 from BMW, which was available to ordinary mortals starting only in 1996. The Z3 also had the honor of being the first new model to be manufactured in BMW's American plant in Spartanburg, South Carolina, which opened in 1994. The first cars made there were equipped with 1.8- and 1.9-liter four-cylinder engines. However, the model with a six-cylinder engine and 2.8-liter displacement was added to the model range in the same year.

Aston Martin vs. Ferrari

An Unequal Duel in *GoldenEye*

77

James Bond is on the road in a DB5 in the hinterlands of Monaco, accompanied by a psychologist who is supposed to assess his fitness for duty. Everything looks like a cozy picnic, but then Xenia Onatopp pops up in the rearview mirror. She is driving a brand-new red Ferrari F355 GTS.

Xenia Onatopp in a Ferrari F355 GTS and James Bond—of course in a Aston Martin DB5—clash on this serpentine road in the hinterlands of Monaco. Bond's car has the license number BMT 214 A; on Sean Connery's car it was 216. *Image: Aston Martin*

Much to the chagrin of a group of cyclists and other travelers on the road, the two cars run a wild race along the narrow twisting road. This is a test of strength between the thirty-year-old English sports car and a brand-new Italian powerhouse. The duel between these two opponents would be repeated several more times during the movie. The model for this race is the one in *Goldfinger* when Bond's car is competing with Tilly Masterson in her white Mustang. On the orders of the psychologist, Brosnan stops immediately because, as he explains, he has no problem with female authority.

The Ferrari F355 GTS

Production period:	1994
Power output:	279 kW
Length:	167.3 inches (4,250 mm)
Height:	46 inches (1,170 mm)
Width:	74.8 inches (1,900 mm)
Top speed:	183 mph (295 km/h)

Bungee Jumping Becomes Popular

007 Jumping a Special Kind of Rope

78

In 1995, Pierce Brosnan makes a very spectacular entrance in his role as James Bond in *GoldenEye*. On a mission that takes him and his colleague 006 to northern Russia, they are supposed to destroy a Soviet chemical weapons factory in the city of Arkhangelsk. Since there is neither a chemical plant nor a dam in this city on a flat coast, the film team moved to Switzerland to film the scene at the Verzasca Dam on the Lago di Vogorno reservoir in the Swiss canton of Ticino. Given that the dam is 722 feet (220 meters) high, it is no joke. It was ideally suited for the shots in the movie's opening sequence, in which Bond makes a bungee jump in order to gain access into the building complex of the forbidden factory. This scene was honored as the best stunt scene of all time.

View of the Verzasca Dam on Lago di Vogorno, where part of the opening sequence was filmed. *Image: I. Rasche / Pixelio.de*

Do It Yourself, Bond!

After the movie was made, two brothers and their company set up a facility at this dam that allows daring fans to perform Bond-style jumps themselves. The depth of the jump actually did set a world record, after all. Anyone who wants to try it out can find everything there is to know on the internet at www.trekking.ch/bungy.

But why Arkhangelsk, a port city where there is no access through the mountains? Maybe it is because the Verzasca Dam structure is what is called an "arch dam"? Or did the Russian city's coat of arms offer a role model? The coat of arms displays the archangel Michael leaping from a lofty height on top of an evil devil.

The High-Tech BMW Brand

79

In a BMW 750iL, the Driver Never Dies

Tomorrow Never Dies is a festival for BMW! The Bavarian car manufacturer took the opportunity to buy into the movie's makers and was able to present its product in a spectacular way. After Q had delivered the new BMW 750iL in the guise of a rental car, the vehicle was quickly given the opportunity to show off all that it could deliver. The car, with its V-12 engine, is attacked by the villains. The sequence recalls the old *Superbug* movies, which were West German children's movies from the 1970s that featured a talented Volkswagen Beetle. The clever VW Beetle, named Dudu, has lots of gadgets. The man who owned Dudu was of course named Jimmy Bondi.

James Bond's own BMW features **gadgets** such as electrodes that emit electric shocks in the door handles, tear gas jets, and indestructible titanium armor. Bond is able to preserve his car and go on the run. This sequence displays gadgets such as tires that repair themselves and onboard missiles. In reality, some seventeen BMW 740iL vehicles were used to make the shoot, and eight of them ended up on the scrap heap afterward.

A battery of missiles peek out from under the sunroof of Bond's new company car.
Image: Morio / CC BY-SA 3.0

The BMW 750iL

Production period:	1994–2001
Power output:	240 kW
Length:	211.6 inches (5,374 mm)
Height:	56.5 inches (1,435 mm)
Width:	73.3 inches (1,862 mm)
Top speed:	155 mph (250 km/h)

Q's BMW—a Self-Driving Car

Remote Control from the Back Seat

In the movie *Tomorrow Never Dies*, James Bond steers his BMW by remote control. To save the car and himself from the villains, 007 uses the remote control to open the rear side window, then jumps into the car and steers it while lying down on the back seat. At the end, Bond jumps out of the back seat and steers the car over the edge of the parking-garage roof and down into the street. Of course, he could not care less about the passersby on the street. The BMW crashes into the window of a car rental company on Mönckebergstrasse in Hamburg. It turns out to be the same one where Q—wearing the Avis company uniform—had handed the car over to James Bond. So the 750iL returns home in one piece.

Later in the movie, 007 shows once again what a good motorcycle driver he is. He has Chinese secret agent Wai Lin as a competent passenger along with him, and he uses her help to eliminate any number of pursuers, eventually even including a helicopter.

This movie is all about the power of the media and, above all, the great danger posed by "fake news." It is bursting with technical gadgetry, revisiting many elements from old movies, such as Karl Stromberg's *Atlantis*, which becomes Elliot Carver's stealth boat.

An ingenious idea of the filmmakers turns James Bond's BMW into a spectacle in *Tomorrow Never Dies*. In the movie, Bond steers his car with his cell phone; in reality, a driver had all the equipment shown here to drive the BMW 750. Of course, he got out before the car makes its leap into the Avis display window. *Image: Me/Pixelio.de*

A glimpse behind the scenes: This is how driving scenes are filmed. Pierce Brosnan in his BMW Z8 knows how to work with the cameras. *Image: BMW/Newspress*

The BMW Z8

Once Again, the Bavarians Deliver the Company Car

81

The World Is Not Enough is the third movie that features a BMW as 007's company car. It was in this movie that the silver roadster was presented to a wide audience for the first time. It was not launched on the market until a year later. The **gadgets**: titanium armor, missiles, and steering by remote control. The end of Bond's Z8 is as unlovely as it is spectacular: the villains slice it into two halves, using circular saw blades they have suspended from a helicopter. James Bond's reaction: "Q is not going to like this!" Once again, 007 has failed to return his equipment in one piece.

The BMW Z8	
Production period:	2000–2003
Power output:	294 kW
Length:	173.2 inches (4,400 mm)
Height:	51.6 inches (1,310 mm)
Width:	72 inches (1,830 mm)
Top speed:	155 mph (250 km/h)

The Tragic Figure of Elektra King

The Bond Girl as 007's Main Enemy

82

In the ancient Greek tragedy, Elektra is a young woman who kills her stepfather and her mother because they have killed her own father. Elektra is also the name of the daughter of the industrialist Sir Robert King, who is murdered at the beginning of the movie *The World Is Not Enough*; he was a friend of M. A terrorist named Renard, who appears to be the movie's primary villain, kidnapped Elektra to extort a ransom. Her father had consulted with M and, on her advice, did not pay it. Elektra tells James Bond, who has been newly assigned to protect her, that she gained her freedom by seducing Renard. Is she suffering from Stockholm syndrome?

The First Woman to Be the Primary Villain

In reality, her father's refusal to pay the ransom had destroyed her world. She never wanted to feel that she was powerless again. That is why she is now seeking omnipotence. The traitors, her father and her quasi-stepmother M—in a reversal of the ancient theme—have to be eliminated. But she makes a crucial mistake, something that she would never have done if she had seen a couple of

This Rolls-Royce Silver Shadow served as the mobile base of operations for the former KGB man Zukowsky. An encounter with Elektra King would become his undoing. *Image: Newspress*

Come, Sweet Death! (J. S. Bach). There are undoubtedly substantially more unpleasant ways of meeting death than encountering it with Sophie Marceau, playing Elektra King, on your lap. *Image: Picture Alliance / Capital Pictures*

Bond movies: she would have known that Bond is certainly very capable of killing her, and that he would do it despite the fact that he was very fond of her. Sophie Marceau is enchanting in this movie and certainly outshines the good-humored Robert Carlyle and also Denise Richards, who plays Christmas Jones.

A Farewell and a New Beginning

The movie was the last one in which Desmond Llewelyn plays Q. He was killed in an auto accident after filming was completed. As if it were a premonition, the legendary Monty Python actor John Cleese had been suggested as his potential successor with the code name R, which "comes right after Q."

Brosnan as 007 kills the fewest people in this movie: twenty-seven, as opposed to the record of forty-seven in *GoldenEye*. The table on the right also shows the average number of casualties per movie and how many flippant quips Bond uttered afterward.

James Bond's Causalities per Actor

Actor	Casualties	Average	Quips
Sean Connery	68	11.33	10
George Lazenby	6	6	1
Roger Moore	121	17.3	9
Timothy Dalton	20	10	2
Pierce Brosnan	103	25.75	6
Daniel Craig	44	14.66	1

A Highland Castle

The Scottish Branch of MI6

83

The World Is Not Enough plays with the origins of James Bond. The title already refers to this, because according to Ian Fleming, this is the motto of the house of Bond. The author had—as 007 himself did in *On Her Majesty's Secret Service*—researched his family in the UK's College of Arms, its official heraldic authority, and came across the coat of arms of Bond of Peckham. On it, he found emblazoned the Latin motto "Orbis non sufficit," which translates to "The world is not enough."

As the movie starts, the MI6 personnel are staying in Scotland so that they can attend the funeral service for M's friend Sir Robert King. Because they have to be able to continue their work, they withdraw to MI6's Scottish base of operations. The castle shown here is an old friend of inveterate movie enthusiasts. Such movies as *Highlander*, *Braveheart*, *Prince Valiant*, and *Rob Roy* all were filmed here. It is the Eilean Donan Castle, located at the confluence of Loch Alsh and two other sea lochs in the Western Highlands, well north of the coastal town of Oban. In the Bond movie, the building is called Castle Thane. When they made the movie, only the exterior shots were filmed there. The interior shots, including all the various technical gadgets, were filmed in the studio.

Eilean Donan Castle, ancestral home of the Scottish Highland Clan MacRae, is a popular Hollywood movie location. In *The World Is Not Enough*, this was the home of the secret headquarters of the Secret Service Scottish Branch. *Image: Rosel Eckstein / Pixelio.de*

An English Duel

The Aston Martin Vanquish and the Jaguar XKR

84

Die Another Day was not only Brosnan's last appearance as James Bond, but also the twentieth movie in the franchise. This milestone was celebrated by indulging in all sorts of reminiscences about the earlier movies. These ranged from allusions to the earlier movies to putting old props back to use—especially in Q's workshop—and to the repetition of elements of various plots. Bond fans have a lot of fun figuring out all of the above, just as they do in searching for movie bloopers. A number of the plot motifs recall the novel version of *Moonraker*. The position held by Gustav Graves is very similar to that of Hugo Drax in the book. He is also very popular and is knighted by the queen. Drax has Gala Brand, an undercover officer of the British Scotland Yard's Special Branch, on his team;

The Jaguar XKR

Production period:	1998–2003
Power output:	276 kW
Length:	187.4 inches (4,760 mm)
Height:	50.7 inches (1,288 mm)
Width:	72 inches (1,830 mm)
Top speed:	155 mph (250 km/h)

The green Jaguar convertible carried an onboard machine gun that is reminiscent of the weapons used by World War I aircraft. In the planes, the guns were mounted on the upper wing. *Image: Newspress*

The English take on the English: a classically molded Aston Martin up against a rather unusually designed Jaguar in a slippery duel of drivers. *Image: Newspress / Premier Automotive Group*

in *Die Another Day*, it is Miranda Frost of MI6, but she is playing a double game. Actually, Drax is—like Graves—a foreigner with the goal of launching an attack on London. In both cases, Bond gets to know his antagonist at the Blades Club in London. In the novel, it is while they are playing cards; in *Die Another Day*, it is during a fencing match.

A Fireworks Display of Action on the Ice and Snow

This movie is a veritable fireworks display of action, starting with the spectacular surfboard ride down the wave in the opening sequence and including the terrifically staged fencing match between Graves and Bond, which certainly does not pale in comparison with Errol Flynn's sword duels. There is no question about the highlight, however; it is the spectacular chase across the frozen lagoon on the Icelandic ice, during which the Aston Martin Vanquish (see page 162) has the opportunity to show off all it can do. The movie's top auxiliary bad guy, Zao, pursues 007 in a Jaguar roadster, which is equipped not only with a machine gun mounted on the windshield frame but also with some onboard missiles, as you can readily see in the image at left. They protrude from the radiator grille. The highlight—which may even be too much of a good thing for many fans—is the Aston Martin's stealth function. It is thanks to this feature that Bond is able to free himself from his troublesome pursuer and save Jinx and the world.

Brosnan's Aston Martin

85

The Aston Martin V-12 Vanquish

This Aston Martin model didn't want to wait until the premiere of the latest 007 adventure. It had already been presented at the Geneva Motor Show in March 2001. The Vanquish was voted one of the most beautiful cars of all time. It had a superpowerful V-12 engine with its four valves per cylinder and 6 liters of engine displacement, but the price would take your breath away: around a quarter of a million dollars. For that price, you could feel like James Bond—but without his **gadgets**.

Q Makes Things Exciting: The Staged Briefing

Q manages to pull off a brilliant move in the way he presents the V-12 Vanquish—in the MI6 special "Vanish" model. He does it in the fictional Vauxhall Cross station of the London Underground; the scenes actually feature Aldwych station, which has been abandoned for years and is very popular for filming. The Vauxhall Cross name makes sense, however, because the MI6 building is not far from Vauxhall Rail Station, located in the London district of the same name, and the bridge that you always see in the movie (see page 53) is the Vauxhall Bridge.

The British Motor Industry Heritage Trust

The British Motor Museum has its home in the village of Gaydon, England, which lies between Birmingham and London. There are hundreds of old cars on display here; they come from the collections of the British Motor Industry Heritage Trust and the Jaguar Heritage Trust. This is the mecca for all fans of British automotive design, which was once a truly mighty force. Currently, it upholds the Union Jack only in the high-end segment. At the museum you will find, for example, the Aston Martin DB2 owned by British racing driver Stirling Moss; the oldest Land Rover ever, built in 1966, which was owned by the queen; a Riley tricycle from 1899; all sorts of Minis; Morris models; and such gems as a Sunbeam Alpine, a Jensen, and a range of Triumphs. Besides all this, the museum is where the Aston Martin V-12 Vanquish that Q presents to James Bond—in a version with plenty of extra options— in *Die Another Day* is parked.

Heavily armed and fast, the Aston Martin V-12 Vanquish, in the Secret Service "Vanish" model, is well equipped for dealing with even the heaviest bumper-to-bumper traffic. *Image: Newspress*

Both Pierce Brosnan and John Cleese show themselves in peak form in these scenes. For each of them, it would be their last appearance in a James Bond movie. Q calls Bond "Double-O Zero." When Bond tells him, "You know, you're cleverer than you look," Q responds maliciously: "Still, better than looking cleverer than you are!" The scene features these wonderful taunts, as well as a stroll through the laboratory with the old **gadgets** and a new ring that can destroy bulletproof glass. And then there is the "Vanish" feature, which can be retracted for invisibility. All the special equipment makes it necessary for the driver to read a thick manual. Bond tosses it into the air and shoots it down with the car's two machine guns. To this Q responds insultingly, "I wish I could make you vanish." Apparently, some Bond fans had the same wish, because this Bond adventure did not really make the cut among the public and especially with the critics. It is a movie to watch a second time, however, so that you can recognize and love all the hidden nuances.

The Aston Martin Vanquish	
Production period:	2001–2007
Power output:	343 kW
Length:	183.7 inches (4,665 mm)
Height:	51.9 inches (1,318 mm)
Width:	75.7 inches (1,923 mm)
Top speed:	190 mph (306 km/h)

Jinx

In the Thunderbird

86

Halle Berry's appearance on the James Bond big screen was skillfully reminiscent of Ursula Andress's first appearance in *Dr. No*. As an Oscar winner, Berry is perhaps the most prominent Bond girl to date. As a CIA agent, she and 007 save the world together.

As a guest at Gustav Graves's Ice Palace, she drives up in a bright-red Ford Thunderbird and is dressed in a very well-fitting leather suit. She is the frequently presented type of clever secret agent who gets close to Bond on more than a professional level. At first, she always seems to be one step ahead of 007, but in the end—as happened with Holly Goodhead and others—it once again becomes necessary for James Bond to save her from a dangerous situation. As a rule, the reward is not very imaginative because it is always the same: an amorous tête-à-tête to make a happy ending. For 007, driving a Thunderbird would have been out of the question. He didn't like US cars because they have too little personality.

Halle Berry as Jinx, who works for the CIA. Visually, she was certainly an enormous asset. But she also played the role very convincingly.
Image: Newspress

James Bond, the Patriot

The Union Jack Is Omnipresent

Every Bond fan is familiar with the famous opening scene in *The Spy Who Loved Me*—in which 007, after being pursued on skis, plunges into an abyss . . . only a moment later to elegantly float away over it with a parachute displaying the flag of Great Britain. This apparently struck a chord with the much-battered imperial sensibilities of the British, because the Union Jack evoked much applause at the movie premiere. London played a marginal role in the earlier movies and was used only as a setting when Bond reported to M for duty or when he returned there before a mission. That would change with Pierce Brosnan. Now more and more scenes were played out in the capital of the United Kingdom. One example occurs in *The World Is Not Enough*, when the headquarters of MI6 are attacked and Bond chases the perpetrator down the Thames River. London also plays an important role in *Skyfall* and *Spectre*. In the latter movie, the finale even takes place on Westminster Bridge.

"For England" is Bond's watchword, and the phrase is mentioned in some of the movies. Or how about this? "James, I need you!" / "England does also!" At the end of *Skyfall*, Bond is looking over the city and sees Big Ben and the waving Union Jack—the mother country has been saved.

An affront: In *Die Another Day*, the villain Gustav Graves uses a patriotic parachute to jump right in front of the Buckingham Palace so that he can be knighted. Isn't it the case that such appearances should be reserved exclusively for James Bond? *Image: Newspress*

Daniel Craig as James Bond on a Honda CRF 250 L in *Skyfall*. *Image: Newspress*

James Bond's Honda
Through the Bazaar on Two Wheels

88

After *From Russia with Love* and *The World Is Not Enough*, Bond visits the Turkish metropolis of Istanbul for the third time in *Skyfall*. While in the second movie, Bond, in the person of Pierce Brosnan, was making more of a touristy trip armed with a camera and busy saving the world, Daniel Craig shows off more of Bond's athletic side by chasing a mercenary assassin across the rooftops of the Grand Bazaar on a Honda. The motorcycle was a Honda CRF 250 L, a trail bike that has been on the market since 2012. This is a 250-class bike with a single-cylinder engine with electronic fuel injection. The 17 kW motorcycle can reach speeds of 77 mph (124 km/h), though not exactly while running over Turkish roof tiles. These tiles caused even more trouble for the producers, because Turkish newspapers claimed that the stuntmen had damaged the rooftops. The producers called a special press conference to refute the accusations.

James Bond's Childhood

Born in Wattenscheid

89

James Bond was born in Wattenscheid—a town in the German Ruhr region? Not in Scotland? This confused quite a few of 007's followers. But it is true. In 2020, Wattenscheid celebrated the hundredth birthday of James Bond, a child of the city (or of the district, because Wattenscheid has been part of the city of Bochum since 1975). In 1973, John Pearson wrote in his book *James Bond: The Authorized Biography* that James Bond was born there on November 11, 1920. This was because his father was then working for the British Empire in Germany, parts of which had been occupied after World War I.

But as is the case with secret agents, they can change their identities at will. In the novel *You Only Live Twice*, Tiger Tanaka confesses that his nickname comes from the fact that he was born in the year of the tiger, according to Chinese astrology. Bond, on the other hand, was born in the year of the rat. But this points to a birth year of 1924. In *The Living Daylights*, Bond's identity card shows his date of birth as November 10, 1948. And the James Bond played by Daniel Craig was born on April 13, 1968. The man certainly moves with the times!

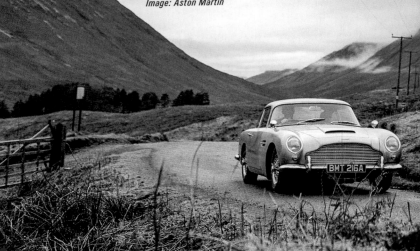

James Bond spent his childhood on the family estate of Skyfall in Scotland, according to the movie of the same name. The gamekeeper Kincade raised him here after his parents died. In his Aston Martin, 007 is no longer very far from Skyfall.
Image: Aston Martin

James Bond's Obituary Sheds Some Light

James Bond's childhood plays a bigger role in *Skyfall*, because the movie's finale takes place at Skyfall, the Scottish Highlands estate where he grew up. An important source for this is the obituary that M wrote in the novel *You Only Live Twice*, when he believed that 007 had died. The obituary states that Bond was brought up exclusively abroad because his father was reported to be a foreign representative of the Vickers engineering company. After his parents' accidental deaths, he was said to have gone to his aunt Charmian Bond's home near Canterbury and then to boarding school at Eton a year later. After harassing a maid there, he reportedly transferred to Fettes College in Edinburgh, where he excelled in boxing and judo. James Bond could not have been any more than eighteen in 1941, because he pretended to be nineteen so that he would be allowed to work for the Navy Department of the Ministry of Defence. By 1945, he had earned the rank of commander and then remained in the secret service, now led by M. Ian Fleming is mentioned as a friend and author of books about him. According to this information, 1924 could be correct as his year of birth, and Bond would have applied to the Navy at age seventeen—Sean Connery joined the navy at sixteen, and Roger Moore joined the Army at eighteen. So, if this is the case, Wattenscheid celebrated Bond's one hundredth birthday a few years early.

The Marketing Train Is Rolling

Beating the Drums—Stirred, Not Shaken

90

The 007 movies are the best-known flicks to use surreptitious advertising. The first such ad is already to be found in *From Russia with Love*, which features a poster advertising another movie made by the producers. This phenomenon had development potential, and it was known to go so far that companies would cooperate closely with EON and release or present their products for the first time in parallel with the movie. James Bond had preferences for certain brands. Ian Fleming always enjoyed mentioning brands in passing in his novels. Most of the time, the agent's tastes coincided with those of his creator. But they couldn't take that into account in the movies. Depending on the advertising partner who was paying, James Bond would accommodate his preferences to them.

The 007 movies always meant a spectacular fireworks display. At the premiere of *Goldfinger*, the movie was also a style setter in terms of advertising: in Paris, the car in which Sean Connery was sitting was escorted by sixty female motorcyclists covered in gold. It must have been an incredible sight to see this convoy parading along the Champs-Élysées. These days, you probably would see a crowd of people like this only when the new iPhone became available somewhere. The DB5 also went on a tour on its own. Fanatics everywhere tried to nab themselves a part of the car. Stars and sheiks absolutely wanted to get the car—at all costs, but without success. Miss Exotica, a stripper from Frisco, had better luck; she at least was allowed to practice her profession on top of the Aston Martin. Whether this made any dents in the vehicle is not known.

007 Earnings *	
Movie Title	**Box Office Gross**
Skyfall	$1,223 million
Thunderball	$1,142 million
Goldfinger	$1,027 million
Spectre	$948 million
Live and Let Die	$929 million
You Only Live Twice	$853 million
The Spy Who Loved Me	$789 million
No Time to Die	$774 million
Casino Royale (2006)	$758 million
Moonraker	$739 million
Diamonds Are Forever	$731 million
Quantum of Solace	$695 million
From Russia with Love	$658 million
Die Another Day	$647 million
On Her Majesty's Secret Service	$608 million
The World Is Not Enough	$597 million
GoldenEye	$592 million
For Your Eyes Only	$569 million
Tomorrow Never Dies	$551 million
The Man with the Golden Gun	$505 million
Dr. No	$503 million
Octopussy	$480 million
The Living Daylights	$429 million
A View to a Kill	$374 million
License to Kill	$321 million

* Adjusted for inflation for better comparability, not the real figures

The Bond advertisement at King's Cross railway station in London. It shows the leading characters in *Skyfall*: M, Séverine, Bond, Moneypenny, and the villain Silva. *Image: Matt Buck / CC BY-S 3.0*

The term "skyfall" evokes a multitude of motifs in the movie. The reference to Christian doctrine is particularly striking. The Christlike figure of 007 falls from the sky (heaven) and is apparently dead. But he celebrates his resurrection and is able to go on the hunt for Lucifer, the villain Silva, who himself once worked on the team of the godlike M but then was allowed to fall from heaven—the next "skyfall"—and takes his revenge. At the end, 007 is victorious, and it is little wonder that the grand showdown at the Bond family Skyfall estate ends in a church.

Earnings from *Skyfall*

With two Academy Awards and box office grosses of $1.1 billion, *Skyfall* is the most successful movie in the franchise to date. The production costs probably ran to something between $150 and $200 million; it is fascinating that some $34 million of this had reportedly been contributed by outside companies, which in return were able to see their products prominently displayed. The table at left shows how much the EON movies grossed at the box office. When looking at these figures, it must be borne in mind that the totals have been calculated on an inflation-adjusted basis to make them more comparable. It should also be borne in mind that movie box office sales were in a crisis during the late 1970s and 1980s.

Moneypenny in the Field

The Modern Woman Also Goes Galavanting

Skyfall brings us a colorful, empowered Moneypenny who works in the field. She actively supports 007 during his mission in Turkey. But when, on orders from M, she has to shoot in a dubious situation, she apparently hits Bond with deadly consequences. She is therefore the one responsible for the fact that 007, for the first time ever, is

unable to complete his mission. In *Die Another Day*, Bond was in fact captured, but he had been able to eliminate his target first. As a result, Moneypenny is put on office duty, working as an assistant to the secret-intelligence coordinator Gareth Mallory, who becomes the new M at the end of the movie (what a pity, since years earlier the author would have wished to see him as James Bond). This is how the constellation that we already know from the Sean Connery movies is created. Eve Moneypenny trusts 007 and helps him secretly, even in dubious circumstances. It will be interesting to see how this relationship develops further. In any case, Bond fans can be happy to see the iconic secretary again after two movies in which they were deprived of her.

Caterpillar takes a curtain call with its successful product placement, while Eve Moneypenny is breaking out in a sweat because she has to be on time for the train. *Image: Newspress*

The Aston Martin DB10

92

Only Ten Were Ever Made and Eight Were for Shooting the Movie

Actually, the DB10 was intended for Bond's colleague 009, but Bond grabs the goods and goes waltzing off in the direction of Italy. In Rome, however, he loses the car after a wild car chase when he is pursued by Hinx in his Jaguar C-X75. The DB10 crashes into the Tiber River, but Bond is able to deploy one of the car's well-known **gadgets**, the ejection seat, and jumps out with his parachute and lands next to a trash collector who scowls at him, befuddled—like something right out of the movies of the Connery-Moore era. It is probably thanks to Daniel Craig, who is also the coproducer, that after some very dark episodes, things are a lot more fun in *Spectre*.

The Aston Martin DB10 was a specially developed car made almost exclusively (see page 182) for the new Bond movie. Compared to the Vanquish, the DB10 is a little narrow chested, because it features only a 4.7-liter V-8 engine. It has 22 kW less power output, but that certainly won't bother anyone. It is highly doubtful that James Bond had ever reached his top speed during the race against Hinx's Jaguar through the nighttime streets of Rome, cordoned off by the police. The well-heeled fans of the secret agent had to content themselves with a special edition of the DB9 (see page 183). By the end of the shoot, the cost of the wear and tear that the moviemakers inflicted on these expensive sports cars reportedly amounted to $48 million. This is a hobby that you first have to be able to afford.

The Aston Martin DB10

Production period:	2014
Power output:	321 kW
Length:	173.6 inches (4,410 mm)
Height:	49.2 inches (1,250 mm)
Width:	76.1 inches (1,934 mm)
Top speed:	193 mph (310 km/h)

Wow! A car that they manufactured just for a movie! The DB10 would never have come into the world if it hadn't been for *Spectre*. Our thanks to James Bond! *Image: Newspress*

Pursuit by Airplane

Sölden's Big Scene in *Spectre*

93

Probably the highlight of the stunts in the fourth Bond adventure starring Daniel Craig, which is not exactly lacking in action, is his pursuit of Madeleine Swann's kidnappers to the mountain clinic at the Geislachkogl mountain gondola station by Sölden, Austria. 007 pursues her in a Britten-Norman BN-2 Islander aircraft that just happens to be standing by. This author has never had the opportunity to even see an airplane there, let alone hijack one, neither in the summer nor in the winter. Fortunately, however, this author's wife hasn't been kidnapped either. Lucky you, Mr. Bond—as happens so often.

It is really fortunate that an airplane just happened to be around right on the Sölden ski slope. This lets Bond effectively pursue the men who kidnapped his girl. *Image: Newspress*

The aircraft, with its original registration of G-BUBG, was flown in from Great Britain especially for the shoot and disguised as OE-FZO (OE for the Ötztal region in Tyrol, Austria). The aircraft was built in 1993 by Pilatus Britten Norman Limited. In *Goldfinger*, the Pilatus factory, located near Lucerne, was used as the main villain's company. Fortunately, Bond doesn't seem to mind that the three cars drive into the Rosi-Mittermaier tunnel—and come out on the same side. During the chase, in any case, the "bird" really got its wings clipped. At least Bond manages to save Madeleine. Thus starts their cooperation, which will later end in a relationship. Bond's relationship with the daughter of the criminal Mr. White, whose end Bond witnesses live during the movie, displays a kind of predatory pattern, not in terms of women to go to bed with, but in terms of women to consider marrying. Tracy Draco Bond, both in the book and the movie *On Her Majesty's Secret Service*, was also the daughter of a criminal.

And . . . Action!

The 007 Franchise and the Movie Directors

94

Most of the studio shoots for making the Bond franchise movie were done at Pinewood Studios, located just outside London. It was there that set designer Ken Adam, who comes from Berlin, built his huge hideouts and palaces for the villains. The interior of Fort Knox in *Goldfinger* lets you forget completely that you have no idea just what it really looks like inside. Adam's successor, Peter Lamont, has been able to maintain the extremely high standards these structures show.

Shooting a James Bond movie is usually some of the most elaborate filming work done in movie history. Spectacular stunts cost time and money, changes to the script take time, and getting the crew from A to B on set is a logistical challenge. The director almost has to be a military field commander to be able to hold the reins in his hands.

These movies keep setting world records. In *Spectre*, it was the biggest blasting operation in movie history. Blofeld's desert headquarters were wiped out by using 73 pounds (33 kilos) of explosives and 2.2 gallons (8.418 liters) of aviation fuel. This corresponds to the equivalent of 68.47 tons of TNT. For comparison: the largest explosion produced by mine warfare during World War I—near the village of Mesen in Belgium—was the equivalent of 225 tons of TNT. The noise could even be heard in London. The movies are always appearance and suggestion. The directors of a 007 flick have to master all this, and their team has to function at a high level.

The Directors

William H. Brown Jr.	*Casino Royale* (1954)
Terence Young	*Dr. No* *From Russia with Love* *Thunderball*
Guy Hamilton	*Goldfinger* *Diamonds Are Forever* *Live and Let Die* *The Man with the Golden Gun*
John Huston/ Ken Hughes/ Robert Parrish/Joseph McGrath/Val Guest	*Casino Royale* (1967)
Peter Hunt	*On Her Majesty's Secret Service*
Lewis Gilbert	*You Only Live Twice* *The Spy Who Loved Me* *Moonraker*
John Glen	*For Your Eyes Only* *Octopussy* *A View to a Kill* *The Living Daylights* *License to Kill*
Irvin Kershner	*Never Say Never Again*
Martin Campbell	*GoldenEye* *Casino Royale* (2006)
Roger Spottiswoode	*Tomorrow Never Dies*
Michael Apted	*The World Is Not Enough*
Lee Tamahori	*Die Another Day*
Marc Forster	*Quantum of Solace*
Sam Mendes	*Skyfall* *Spectre*
Cary Joji Fukunaga	*No Time to Die*

A glimpse behind the scenes. This was taken just as they are filming Bond's pursuit of the cars driven by Hinx and his men after they kidnapped Dr. Madeleine Swann. The camera is well protected. *Image: Newspress*

Oscars and Awards

007 got his first award in 1964: Ursula Andress won a Golden Globe for the Most Promising Newcomer—Female. The Oscar that *Goldfinger* won in 1965 meant great cinema, even if it was only for Best Sound Effects. In 1966, *Thunderball* won the Oscar for Best Visual Effects. George Lazenby was nominated for the 1970 Golden Globe for Most Promising Newcomer—Male. In 1974, Paul McCartney and Wings were nominated for a Grammy for their theme song. In 2000, Denise Richards accomplished the feat of earning a Worst Actress award and a Best Actress nomination in different contests. For *Skyfall*, Adele won both a Golden Globe and an Oscar for her title song. An Oscar also went to Per Hallberg for the Best Sound Editing. It had been a long dry spell since *Thunderball*. Sam Smith surprisingly repeated Adele's 2016 Golden Globe and Oscar feat for his theme song for *Spectre*.

A Cinematic Installation for Bond

95

In 1969, Ernst Stavro Blofeld was running a mental hospital in the Swiss Alps, where luscious young women under the domination of Irma Bunt are prepared for a life without complexes. In reality, they were supposed to carry a pathogen with them in perfume bottles and distribute it in response to a hypnotic command. In 2015, the ICE Q, a restaurant on Geislachkogl mountain, near Sölden in Austria, was transformed into the Hoffler Klinik. Ian Fleming came to love Austria very much after he spent a long time in the mountain town of Kitzbühel in Tyrol and set several of his books in the Alpine country.

A High-Tech Museum Dedicated to James Bond

For Sölden itself, the filming of *Spectre* had lasting consequences in the form of the creation of the 007 ELEMENTS Cinematic Installation—9,974 feet (3,040 meters) high, atop and inside the summit of the Gaislachkogl in Sölden. The modern, two-story building was erected right next to the ICE Q restaurant, which was used for the Hoffler Klinik in the movie. You enter the exhibition to the sound of James Bond music, through a tunnel that re-creates the famous opening scene looking down a gun barrel. Visitors can experience the movie *Spectre* in a multimedia installation distributed over

mme rooms. The most impressive object in the 007 ELEMENTS is certainly the wreckage of the Britten-Norman BN-2 Islander (see page 176). Director Sam Mendes and Moneypenny actress Naomie Harris talk about shooting the movie and the 007 franchise. In one of the rooms, visitors can follow the exact progress of the airplane and car chase that was filmed outside in the fantastic Tyrolean landscape.

Digitization 007

Of course, a cinematic installation means acoustics and big screens above all. The interactive high-tech galleries present title sequences and dramatic soundscapes from various Bond movies. 007 ELEMENTS shows them all—the action scenes, cars, and gadgets. You get a behind-the-scenes look at the filming locations and studio sets and the technical finesse used to create the movie scenes and stunts. The Bond fan experiences iconic dialogues and scenes from the movies, presented in a new way. One highlight is the digital archive made available by the production company EON, where visitors can dive deep into the fascinating adventure world of 007 via touchscreen.

Bond fans will enjoy a trip to Sölden—even if they don't ski—if they stop by the James Bond 007 ELEMENTS Cinematic Installation on Gaislachkogl (*at left*) (the mountain summit station for the gondola!). At right and clad in black is the ICE Q restaurant. *Image: Newspress*

Commerce and Charity

Bond's Company Car Goes under the Hammer

96

Aston Martin manufactured just ten DB10 cars in total. Eight of them were used for shooting the movie, with two left over that were used only for show purposes. One of these was furnished with a plaque signed by Daniel Craig and transported to Christie's auction house in London. It was sold at auction on February 18, 2016. The hammer fell for a sale price amounting to 2,434,500 British pounds—which was more than $3 million. This sum was transferred to Doctors Without Borders, a humanitarian medical organization. The new owner is unknown.

Dedicating the car to this charitable purpose actually makes a lot of sense, because Dr. Madeleine Swann had spent some time working for Doctors Without Borders. The organization, which was awarded the Nobel Peace Prize in 1999, was founded in 1971 exactly one week after the premiere of *Diamonds Are Forever*. It is involved in humanitarian projects in disaster areas all over the world.

This 007 Aston Martin DB10 was auctioned off for a charitable cause. However, the car isn't registered for road driving. *Image: Newspress*

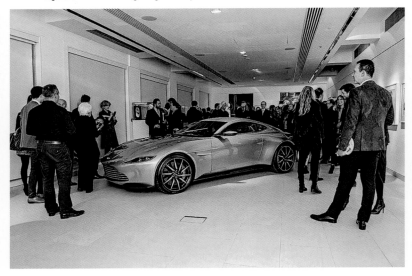

The DB10 wasn't launched on the market; instead, wealthy 007 fans were offered a Bond Edition of the DB9 GT on the occasion of the *Spectre* premiere. *Image: Newspress*

The Car for the Fans

The Aston Martin DB9 GT Bond Special Edition

It was of no use even to those who would easily have $3 million in cash to play around with: the DB10 was never put on the market. Aston Martin was able to appease the hungry Bond fans, however, and instead offered them the DB9 GT in a special James Bond Edition. This certainly did not disappoint horsepower enthusiasts, because this car accommodates a big V-12 engine under the hood. This means it has an increased power output of 81 kW in comparison to the DB10; thus exactly 111 horsepower. This special edition was limited to 150 cars and featured 007 design elements. The price was significantly lower than what the DB10 achieved at auction—$240,000, and it comes with some gadgets, just as the Omega Seamaster 007 Edition does (see page 30).

97

The Aston Martin DB9 GT	
Production period:	2015/2016
Power output:	402 kW
Length:	185.4 inches (4,710 mm)
Height:	52 inches (1,320 mm)
Width:	73.8 inches (1,875 mm)
Top speed:	183 mph (295 km/h)

Bond Cars You Can Play With

Corgi and Lego Accommodate 007 Fans

The most-famous James Bond cars have been finding their way into children's toy chests since *Goldfinger*. The Sears company offered a model car racetrack for running cars such as models of the DB5. In 1965, the Corgi company came out with its first die-cast zinc alloy model cars, based on cars from movies and TV series. The first model was the P1800 driven by *The Saint*'s Simon Templar (see page 27), followed by the bestselling Aston Martin DB5. When *Spectre* came out, this model was sold in a set of two along with the DB10. Other Corgi models included the Lotus Esprit and the Citroën Duck from *For Your Eyes Only*.

Lego makes a 1,295-piece model of the DB5 that you can put together yourself—something for the young at heart. Many Bond fans certainly grew up with Lego and are sure to have fun with it—and, of course, the gadgets are included. This Lego Creator series also includes models of the VW Bus, VW Beetle, a London double-decker bus, and a Swiss "crocodile" railroad locomotive.

Corgi's tradition of making Bond model cars is almost as old as the movies themselves. The set with DB5 and DB10 came out along with *Spectre*. Image: Aston Martin

LEGO CREATOR

EXPERT

A super "professional" DB5 model kit from the Danish toymaker giant. *Images: Aston Martin*

The James Bond Triumph

The British Motorcycle Manufacturer Is Part of the Action

It seems that *No Time to Die* wasn't born under a lucky star. Besides all the turbulence around the script, the roles of movie music composer and director also changed hands. Actor Daniel Craig and a member of the film crew were injured on the set—and Craig had been reluctant for some time to take on the role again, something we have come to expect from Bond actors since the Sean Connery era. And, just when they finally had everything in the can, the COVID-19 pandemic struck.

Something for Everyone?

Once again, this movie was not based on any Ian Fleming title, although it makes use of motifs from *You Only Live Twice* and *On Her Majesty's Secret Service*. However, it is said that a great deal of material had been drawn from the Bond novel *Never Dream of Dying* by American author Raymond Benson. That sounds confusing,

The completely new Tiger 900 delivered a brilliant performance during the shooting. Triumph sent three prototypes to the film team. *Image: Triumph*

Lee Morrison was the rider who performed Bond's motorcycle stunts in *No Time To Die*. Here is a take on set that shows the camera tracks as well as the many people who assist the work to create such a scene. *Image: Triumph*

because neither the locations nor any of the names match up. In any case, the idea was to include more humor in the movie and all kinds of action.

Triumph Brings a Motorcycle to the Table

The British secret agent finally gets to ride an English motorcycle. Triumph, the legendary maker of two wheelers, is an official partner of 007 and has contributed the Tiger 900 and the Scrambler 1200 XE for shooting the movies. For certain, everyone already knows that a Triumph 900 can perform daring stunts when the rider really pushes his bike hard. Triumph reports that their cooperation will be extended beyond this movie. Triumph had brought out its first Tiger by 1936, by the way.

The Triumph Tiger 900	
Production period:	from 2021
Power output:	70 kW
Engine displacement:	888 cm3
Height:	55.5–57.5 inches (1,410–1,460mm)
Wheelbase:	61.25 inches (1,556 mm)
Top speed:	top secret

The New Bond Vehicles

The Aston Martin DBS Superleggera and Valhalla

No Time to Die is, in any case, an Aston Martin festival. The two cars made by this auto maker that have driven the most-spectacular missions in the 007 movies make their appearance: the DB5 and the V-8 Vantage from *The Living Daylights*. But, of course, there is also something new—two vehicles this time, in fact. The first model is the DBS Superleggera. The first cars of this model were already available for purchase by 2018. To mark the fiftieth anniversary of *On Her Majesty's Secret Service* in 2019, a limited special edition of fifty cars was manufactured, as the OHMSS Special Edition. In celebration of the premiere of the new movie, Aston Martin

The DBS Superleggera

Production period:	since 2018
Power output:	533 kW
Length:	185.5 inches (4,712 mm)
Height:	50.4 inches (1,280 mm)
Width:	77.5 inches (1,968 mm)
Top speed:	211 mph (340 km/h)

A photo opportunity for the DBS Superleggera together with the DB11 (*right*). *Image: Aston Martin*

Aston Martin's Valhalla was created in collaboration with Red Bull Racing. *Image: Aston Martin*

released a 007 Edition—which is in some ways modeled on the movie vehicle—of twenty-five cars, in honor of the twenty-five Bond movies. The DBS Superleggera has a newly developed V-12 engine with an engine displacement of 5.2 liters. It accelerates to 62 mph (100 km/h) in just 3.4 seconds.

From the Realm of the Fallen Warriors

In July 2019, the Aston Martin Valhalla was spotted for the first time in Scotland while the new movie was being filmed. The vehicle has a 865 kW sister model with a V-12 engine called the Valkyrie, a name that also comes from Norse mythology. The Valhalla is supposed to be equipped with only a V-6 engine. Both are hybrid models with an additional electric motor. A Valkyrie is said to cost $3 million, with the Valhalla in the neighborhood of $1.3 million. Bond fans interested in seeing what the Valhalla can do in action will be a bit disappointed, however, since the car has only a brief cameo in the film. It appears in one scene and is not mentioned by name or driven. At least that means that it did not suffer the damage 007's exploits often inflict on his vehicles!

It All Comes Full Circle

James Bond Is Back in Jamaica

"You and your Jamaica!" This is what Bond's French colleague René Mathis sneers at him in the novel version of *Casino Royale*. 007 and this island: it's a special relationship. After *Spectre*, James Bond has turned his back on MI6 and immigrated to Jamaica. The character of secret agent James Bond had been born on this very Caribbean island in 1952. This is where Ian Fleming created all of his 007 stories.

So it is fitting that Bond is enjoying a tranquil life in Jamaica—having left active service—when the action begins in *No Time to Die*. His peaceful break is short lived, since a friend from the CIA turns up to enlist his help, setting off an adventure to track down a mysterious villain armed with dangerous new technology. The final movie of Daniel Craig's reign as Bond features plenty of the usual 007 staples: fast cars, pretty women, fancy gadgets, and wild action sequences. But it also blazes new ground and includes a truly shocking ending: James Bond, the seemingly indestructible 007, dies!

Waiting for Number 26

The waiting time between *Spectre* and *No Time to Die* was by far the longest between two Bond movies. Those were the days, when Sean Connery filmed one almost every year! At least when *No Time to Die* finally arrived,

COVID-19, the Bond Antagonist

COVID-19 is perhaps Bond's most dangerous opponent to date. More insidious than Blofeld, faster than Scaramanga, and greedier than Goldfinger. The problems that developed during the filming of *No Time to Die* had made the originally planned premiere in November 2019 impossible anyway. The debut was finally supposedly to come in April 2020, but the launch of the film was delayed by the coronavirus pandemic. It was initially postponed to November and then again to March 2021 before finally making its long-awaited premiere in movie theaters on October 8, 2021.

it provided moviegoers with plenty of material: clocking in at 163 minutes, the film has the longest run time for a Bond movie.

With Daniel Craig's Bond tenure ending in a blaze of glory, the next film in the franchise—the twenty-sixth adventure of 007—will need a new leading actor, and speculation over who will next portray the iconic spy is intense. Who will it be? Idris Elba (who has already gained experience in the security field in his series *Luther*), making Bond a Black man? Or Tom Hardy, who as Mad Max knows all about the experience of having to reinterpret a familiar character? Michael Fassbender, a car fanatic who was born in Germany like James Bond? Tom Hiddleston, who has already played a secret agent in a television series? Robert Pattinson, already a veteran of the Twilight and Batman franchises? Or perhaps someone entirely different? Are you already excited?

In a Range Rover Series III—of course, a right-hand drive—Daniel Craig shows himself as James Bond in (non)retirement. It's the calm before the storm. *Image: Newspress*

For Marlon, who would certainly like this book if he could already read and who will definitely be a big Bond fan one day.

Author: Michael Dörflinger
Product manager: Lothar Reiserer
Composition: Azurmedia, Augsburg, Germany
Cover design: Molly Shields

Secret agent art (cover, pp. 60, 92): Birsen Cebeci/Shutterstock.com
Octopus art (cover, p. 3): Aritha/Shutterstock.com
Cracks in glass art: Vladimirkarp/Shutterstock.com

ISBN: 978-0-7643-6517-1
Printed in India
Type Set In: Garamond/Frutiger/Univers

Published by Schiffer Publishing, Ltd.
4880 Lower Valley Road
Atglen, PA 19310
Phone: (610) 593-1777
Fax: (610) 593-2002
Email: Info@schifferbooks.com
Web: www.schifferbooks.com

Schiffer Publishing's titles are available at special discounts for bulk purchases for sales promotions or premiums. Special editions, including personalized covers, corporate imprints, and excerpts, can be created in large quantities for special needs. For more information, contact the publisher.